ONE FAMILY, ONE STATE, ONE PEOPLE

A Family History and Memoir

ONE FAMILY, ONE STATE, ONE PEOPLE

Renaissance in Mississippi

Marjorie N Cowan

One Family, One State, One People
Renaissance in Mississippi
A Family History and Memoir

ISBN: 979-8-9944952-1-6 (eBook)
ISBN: 979-8-9944952-0-9 (Print)

Copyright:

1-15086567850

Author Photograph Credit: Kymani Raymond

Printed in the United States of America
First Edition

For more information or inquiries contact the author

Thank you for your cooperation

DEDICATION

To my grandchildren: Kymani and Kareem, Kadija, Alpha and Abdul-Rahim, Aaminah, Zariah and Carlissa, and to Yasmeen. To the paths that they will blaze among the stars and the souls they will reach back to help along the way.

For my Family:

"A family is like a forest, when you are outside it is dense, when you are inside you see that every tree has its place."

"However far a stream flows, it doesn't forget its origin."

"If you want to know the end, look at the beginning."

-African Proverbs

THE MAPP FAMILY TREE

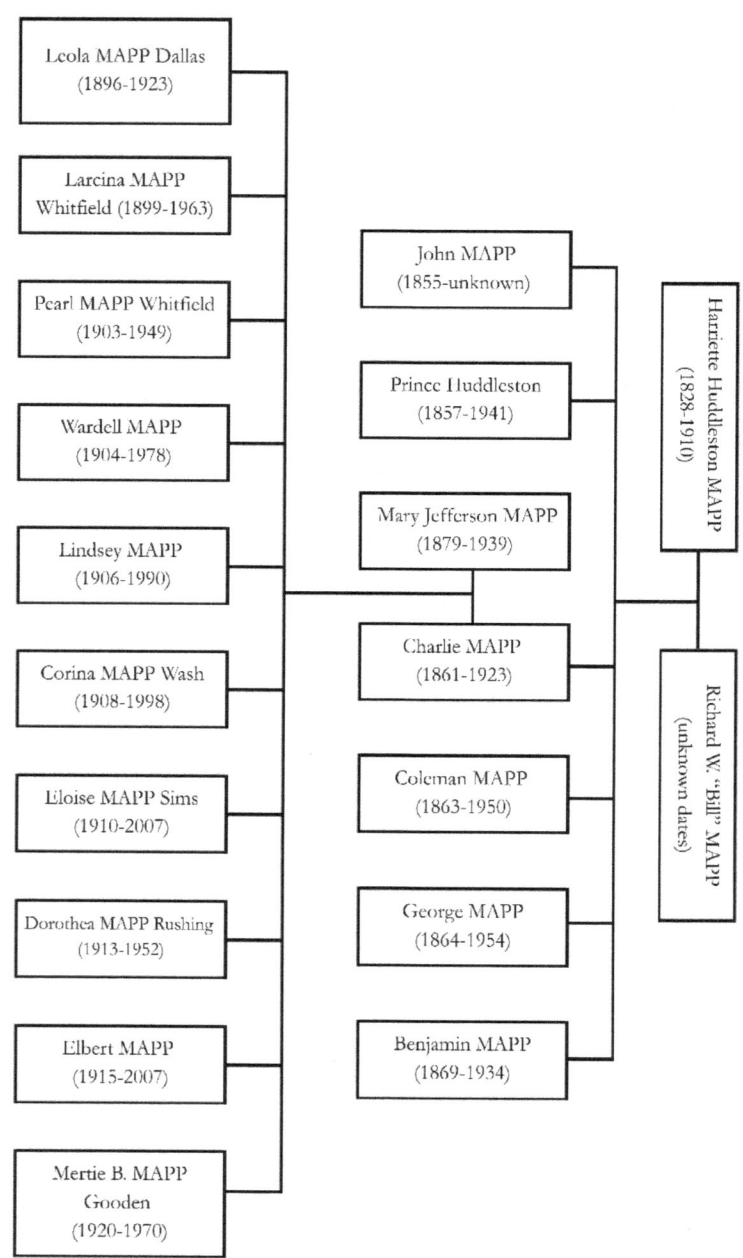

Leola MAPP Dallas
(1896-1923)

Larcina MAPP
Whitfield (1899-1963)

Pearl MAPP Whitfield
(1903-1949)

Wardell MAPP
(1904-1978)

Lindsey MAPP
(1906-1990)

Corina MAPP Wash
(1908-1998)

Lloise MAPP Sims
(1910-2007)

Dorothea MAPP Rushing
(1913-1952)

Elbert MAPP
(1915-2007)

Mertie B. MAPP
Gooden
(1920-1970)

John MAPP
(1855-unknown)

Prince Huddleston
(1857-1941)

Mary Jefferson MAPP
(1879-1939)

Charlie MAPP
(1861-1923)

Coleman MAPP
(1863-1950)

George MAPP
(1864-1954)

Benjamin MAPP
(1869-1934)

Harriette Huddleston MAPP
(1828-1910)

Richard W. "Bill" MAPP
(unknown dates)

ACKNOWLEDGEMENTS

First and foremost I give thanks to Almighty Allah for guiding me, giving me the inspiration, courage and the health to begin and to endure until the completion of this work. I am grateful for the team of angels He sent to assist me, without which I would not have been able to finish. The first angels were my mother and father who gave my brothers, sisters, and me a loving childhood. I thank Allah daily for their love and encouragement.

My daughter Aqueelah Barrie was my number one supporter in all aspects of this project: she initiated and helped to implement all the genealogy research, attended numerous seminars, webinars and Zoom meetings to learn more about the process of family history research, and encouraged me to publish our findings. She never gave up during the periods when we seemed to hit brick walls. Aqueelah has done tremendous work and acquired expertise which could easily be transferred to help others who are seeking their own family history.

There are many others I would like to thank for their encouragement and for rolling up their sleeves to help when needed. You are all so much appreciated. A few in particular are my sister Claudia Jones and my brother Will Amos, who both read first drafts of the book and provided helpful feedback. Thank you Will for going the extra mile to restore a vintage photo of our parents to include in the book, an excellent job and heartfelt gesture.

I also thank my sister Vicky Amos, who provided some timely and much needed technical support. Special thanks go to my brother Jimmy Amos for guiding me to some historic cemeteries to capture photos of ancestors' gravestones.

Also for technical support my daughter Aishah Cowan spent many hours scanning documents, creating needed databases and digital photo files. I am so grateful for her help.

The following two individuals helped tremendously with editing and structure: Wafiyyah Luqman and Naimah Sudan. Their remarkable insight, suggestions and feedback were invaluable in assisting me to move closer to the finish line.

My sincere thanks and appreciation go to the relatives who provided oral history information or other support: Lynn Hunt, the late Percy Reese, Jabari Mapp, Eva Rodgers, and the late Leon Huddleston.

Thank you so much to those who provided family photos: Pat Gooden, Wilbur Sims, Yolanda Gooden, Rochelle Wash, Jo Rushing, Pat Blaylock, Al Malone, Lucia Sims, Pam Gill and Dora Alexander. Special thanks go to my cousin Sandra Whitfield Smith for her cherished photos and her encouragement from the start to finish.

Thank you so much to those relatives who I first met online, those who shared and supported my passion for genealogy, especially Bridget Heard and Calvin Morrow. All of the extended family support meant so much to me.

To my entire immediate family, thank you for your loving patience and support during this entire process, which turned out to be a long haul: to my husband Duane; to my adult children, Shadeed, Aqueelah, Aishah, Sahira, and Faizah; to the memory of my son Kareem; to my grandchildren; and to my siblings and their spouses. Thank you all and I love you dearly.

And finally, I thank all those relatives and friends who encouraged me with their positive energy and who boosted my confidence by believing in me.

All of you above were my team of 'angels' sent by the Almighty. Thank you ever so much.

CONTENTS

INTRODUCTION

This work is only the beginning of a dialogue that I hope will spark the curiosity and interests of our younger generations. In my vision a group of our youth will take up this torch and expand upon its humble beginnings. This book only scratches the surface of our family's very wide network.

It is my prayer that younger generations will solve some of the remaining genealogy mysteries, and break down brick walls and barriers, which remain unsolved here. Those future contributions will allow a fuller, unobstructed view of the challenges, heroism and majesty of our family, our culture and our history.

Included here is a brief history of the state of Mississippi, an overview of slavery, Jim Crow laws, and the Civil Rights struggle primarily for the benefit of our youth. As Americans we all realize that the truly authentic history of this country has not been taught in our schools. So this is an attempt to provide some information to fill that void and possible lack of knowledge. Also I wanted to provide background and context of the conditions and circumstances of our family members as they struggled to make better lives for themselves during their times.

When my daughter Aqueelah and I started this project, our primary goal was to trace our family roots and family ties as far back as possible, back through segregation, Jim Crow, Reconstruction, slavery and finally back to our tribe in AFRICA!!!

We started out with some oral history information and unfortunately even fewer paper records. However, I had grown up in a family network which was very close-knit and included a wide circle: my aunts, uncles, cousins, in-laws and other relatives and family friends.

Our family story begins in Mississippi, a Southern state which offers great beauty in its natural resources. It has rich farmland and pine forests, creeks and streams; the cool, clear water springs from my childhood memories; and even white sand beaches on its Gulf Coast.

However, for much of my lifetime, Mississippi has shown up near the bottom in economics, education, and industry in the United States. It is a state where half of the population, mainly African-Americans, had been subjected to racial discrimination from the Reconstruction era in the 1890s until the Civil Rights Movement in 1965. This was racial discrimination which was not only social, but was enshrined in state laws.

"This is Our-story not HIS-story, told through our own eyes, our own lived experiences, our own blood, sweat and tears... A story to be passed down to future generations"

From me to myself and from me to our grandchildren

But my family's story is about *victory* and not *defeat*. Ours is a story of survival, a story of perseverance, and strength. A story of 'Devil, you can't take my joy.' It's a story of Love and Hope and Patience. My own childhood memories attest to the resilience of our family, and of the African-American people. My childhood was grounded in Love, Hope, and Patience by my parents, my grandparents, and the community.

This narrative will show how my ancestors lived under the long shadow of Jim Crow, survived the Great Depression in the 1930s, and fought for this country during both World War I and World War II. And despite all the obstacles and roadblocks thrown at them from a society built on racial discrimination, my ancestors became the heroes.

This is a story about those heroes, those who survived and thrived in a place which chose to stifle or to ignore them. It is a story of men and women who remained faithful to the Almighty, to their families and to their communities. They fought back against racial oppression by retaining their faith, their dignity, and love for family.

The more family research we did the more I came to realize that the value of this work is the honoring of our ancestors. Through modern DNA advances we were able to learn that my family has origins in Nigeria, Cameroon, and Benin. But the larger story is that our ancestors were heroes, especially once they were brought to America and had to make a life for themselves, battling so many adversities.

It is our job to share the determination, the tenacity and the glory of our ancestors with the younger generations. We will pass on the torch by showing our children and grandchildren what their ancestors accomplished, despite working against extremely heavy odds. We want to show them how their blood survived slavery and its 100-year aftermath of Jim Crow terrorism, including racial oppression and persecution up until the late 1960s. Our families were heroes and their legacy deserves to be honored.

This book's primary goal shifted in the course of the research from identifying an African tribe to testifying about the sacrifices, the faith, and resilience of our ancestors. We want every child to know that our ancestors have provided the foundation on which they can build their own lives and legacies, pushing the boundaries toward even greater achievements.

CHAPTER 1

Mississippi: Heart of the Jim Crow South. A Brief History Review

"...the facts of American history in the last half century have been falsified because the nation was ashamed. The South was ashamed because it fought to perpetuate human slavery. The North was ashamed because it had to call in the black men to save the Union, abolish slavery and establish democracy." **—W.E.B. Du Bois, Black Reconstruction In America 1860-1880**

*O*n a quiet Sunday afternoon we headed home after visiting my grandmother in Newton County, Mississippi. It was the late 1950s and the highways were mostly two-lane, narrow and winding with very little traffic. A three-hour trip felt much longer, especially for a five-year-old.

The road meandered through lots of small towns between the center of the state and the Gulf Coast where we lived. My dad drove a 1949 Chrysler sedan, a huge car with a big, wide cave-like back seat. On a road trip, our car was perfect for four kids to play all the games they wanted, to take a nap or to roll around on the floor. This was back in the days before the United States had even considered seatbelt requirements.

Suddenly we heard a piercing siren that startled the entire family. A red light was flashing from the police car directly behind us. My Dad immediately pulled over on the shoulder, while we children froze in place. Four siblings, all of us under the age of seven. My mom and dad looked very intense, grave but not panicked. However, we kids knew the situation was serious enough that it was not the time to ask questions, squirm or make noises. There was not even a peep from the youngest one, who was probably under two years old.

The state patrol officer strolled up to our car and even though I don't remember what he said to my dad I can imagine it was something demeaning. Daddy handed over his driver's license, following the officer's commands. After a brief conversation my dad was asked to follow the patrolman to the police station. On the inside I began to panic but not daring to express any emotions. Why were we being taken to jail? What was about to happen to Daddy? Would Mama have to drive us home, over two hours away? Or would all of us be locked away somewhere?

We arrived at the police station and my Dad was told to get out of his car and come inside. Still complete silence in the car among us kids. Now my mom looks worried, but she remains quiet and doesn't try to explain anything to us kids. Tears were in our eyes and rolled down our cheeks as we looked down at the floor. We still didn't dare speak. Though we were young we knew instinctively that our family was in crisis.

After what seemed like an eternity, but may have been ten to fifteen minutes Daddy returned to the car. The officer had given him a ticket for *speeding and had fined him an exorbitant amount. My dad had to pay the fine right there on the spot or face being locked up overnight. He would have had to wait until Monday morning to see a judge. We saw Daddy's frustration and Mama's sigh of relief. Her eyes signaled that we were going to be okay.*

In hindsight what is interesting though is the fact that there was no radar detection gear available in that small Mississippi town in the 1950s. The patrolman would have been unable to prove that Daddy was guilty of speeding. But the evidence which the law enforcement officer had against my father was clear and irrefutable: my Dad was driving while Black.

We children learned a lesson that day and had to go home with many unanswered questions lingering in our minds and psyches. Our dad had done nothing wrong but was penalized anyway. We learned that our world was restricted and we had to navigate around the color line, a grim reality that seeped into the hearts and minds of children at a very young age in the South and especially in Mississippi.

There was a time when hearing the word "Mississippi" would bring up strong images and feelings for some people. And for some, those images were not always good ones. People from previous generations, who may have heard about or who may have lived through some painful experiences in the state. Some may have even been haunted by unresolved traumas.

The United States government failed its African-American citizens, especially those living in the South for a long period of time after Reconstruction until the Voting Rights Act of 1965. At that point during the Civil Rights Era, finally some of the savagery being committed against Black people became exposed.

Mississippi was ground zero for racial discrimination, a place which had set the nation's tone for racial violence, terrorism, and its commitment to white supremacy for decade after decade since the Emancipation Proclamation.

There were some incidents of racial violence in the state which became iconic throughout the nation. First, in 1955 there was the murder of Emmett Till, a young Chicago teenager visiting his relatives Down South. A beautiful, promising youth who died for allegedly "whistling" at a young white woman store clerk after he purchased candy or bubble gum. Insanity.

The second murder was a cold-hearted assassination of community activist, military veteran, and NAACP organizer Medgar Evers, who was gunned down in his driveway in front of his wife and young children. His crime against the state of Mississippi: organizing voter registration drives to help black people vote in a place where voting rights had been stripped away from African-Americans despite the 14th Amendment to the US Constitution.

The third incident came at the height of protests, activism, and groundwork by Civil Rights icons, Dr Martin Luther King's Southern Christian Leadership Conference (SCLC), SNCC, and others. This was the 1964 murder of three youth volunteers who were helping to organize black voters in the state of Mississippi and other areas of the South. Goodman, Schwerner, and Chaney were followed by Klansmen, kidnapped and lynched in a wooded area. Two of the men were white college students from Northern cities. The final young man of the threesome was local and was black, and reportedly suffered the most severe torture of the three victims, not surprisingly. After all, the conventional wisdom of "white supremacy" would have been to make an example of a young Black man who grew up in the area, and who had the gall to "get out of line" by demanding his full human rights.

Outcomes of these horrific events: In the till case the perpetrators were acquitted by an all-white jury after a brief trial. To add insult to injury, these men were paid a lump sum of $3500 by *Look Magazine* to appear in the January 1956 issue of that publication. In an article entitled "The Shocking Story of Approved Killing in Mississippi "by reporter William Bradford Huie, the men boasted about their crimes.[1] Much has been written about the Till case, of course, in addition to the production of documentaries and movies. One of the earlier accounts from a courthouse witness to the trial is available in Simeon Booker's *Shocking the Conscience: a Reporter's Account of the Civil Rights Movement*. Booker covered the trial as a reporter for *Jet Magazine* back in 1955.

In the Medgar Evers' assassination, the shooter, Byron DeLa Beckwith was tried and sentenced to life imprisonment in 1994, over thirty years following the killing of the Civil Rights legend. Beckwith had been originally acquitted in 1964. More about Medgar Evers and his coincidental ties to my own family will appear in a later section.

As for the Chaney, Goodman and Schwerner case, which occurred at the height of the Civil Rights Movement, there was a more urgent response. We saw the nation move to hold the perpetrators accountable for the lynching of those three innocent young men.

Due to pressure brought by the White House, under the Lyndon Johnson administration, pressure brought by intense media coverage; and from general public outrage, the state of Mississippi was forced to, or at least make an attempt, to deliver some measure of justice.

However, although local authorities made some arrests in the Fall of 1964, these men were released and no initial indictments were issued. In 1967, three years after the murders, the FBI indicted 18 men on federal charges. Of that number, six were convicted and served 3 - 6 years in prison.

One convicted individual was Sam Bowers, an official Klan wizard. Florence Mars, a white Civil Rights sympathizer and resident of Neshoba

County, where the murders occurred, wrote a detailed account of events surrounding the murders. Her book, entitled Witness in Philadelphia, published in 1977, contains the following:

"The convictions were a turning point for Mississippi. This was the first time a jury In the state had returned a guilty verdict in a major civil rights case since Reconstruction, and ....marked the end of the long chain of widely publicized and unpunished racial killings... State observers 'felt that the convictions would not only restrain terrorist activities... But would also make it easier for the prosecution to obtain verdicts in future cases...."[2]

In 2005, more than forty years after the murders, primary suspect and defendant Edgar Ray Killen was indicted and convicted on state charges. He was sentenced to 60 years in prison for three counts of manslaughter. Killen died in prison in 2018.

Why was justice so long in coming? Part of the reason lies in the origin story of the state of Mississippi, which was founded for the purpose of cultivating the land for the benefit of a handful of owners, the capitalists of the 1800's. And of course their method of extracting wealth from the land was tied and molded to the institution of human trafficking, the institution of chattel slavery. Slavery was how Mississippi began its statehood in the United States, and so must be examined in order to understand the conditions and climate of the state since that time. And to understand future challenges and aspirations.

Slavery in the United States: Staring the Beast in the Eye

So the state of Mississippi indeed has an ugly, and extremely notorious past history. But despite its bitter history, the state of Mississippi is home to millions of African-Americans, millions of Black people. During the height of slavery it has been estimated that about one million black people were transported to the state for the production of cotton. Enslaved peoples who were perhaps born in Virginia or North Carolina were sold to traders who transported them further south, in many cases on foot, walking to their destinations. By the early 1800's landowners, entrepreneurs, and land speculators found new ways to capitalize on the system of human bondage. Because land was plentiful, cheap, and very fertile in the Deep South, the nation's businessmen rushed to cash in on these new opportunities. More enslaved people were sold or traded during this time both to simply make a profit or to conveniently dispose of those enslaved individuals who may have been rebellious, or those who had attempted to escape.

The Half Has Never Been Told by author Edward E. Baptist provides an excellent account of this period of history. Baptist paints a picture of how Americans generally have little factual knowledge about the realities of building a slave economy in the American South.

Nor does the average American want to admit that the nation's slave economy translated to prosperity for the North and solidified the United States as a worldwide economic power.

It is not taught in schools how the wealthy planter class extracted all the life from enslaved people in order to maintain their own wealth. Nor is it taught how human beings walked barefoot in the cold and rain coffle-chained for hundreds, sometimes thousands of miles while being moved from one location to another. Jesmyn Ward's recent (2025) lyrical novel *Let Us Descend* captures the spiritual essence of these forced migrations. Ward follows one young woman's walk from Maryland to a New Orleans slave auction house, which is a three-month ordeal fighting starvation, river-crossings, insect-swarms, and the barbaric cruelty of being shackled to persons before and behind her.

Once reaching their destinations and depending upon the inclination or whims of the owners, these human beings were then fed scantily, housed

11

in ramshackle hovels, worked daily from sunrise till sunset, and in many cases whipped unmercifully if considered disobedient. A great amount of human suffering and carnage occurred to support the massive wealth of a handful of European descendants and their families. This slave-labor generated wealth fed a large portion, over fifty percent, of the total US economy. The cotton produced in Mississippi brought textile factories to the North, and also spurred trade with foreign nations like England and France.

Resistance by Our Enslaved Ancestors

Although the system of slavery in the United States was designed to strip away the humanity of almost five million people at its peak point in 1860, evidence shows that enslaved people found ways to hold on to their God-given right, the humanity of a people. Indeed enslaved people always aspired for freedom. Innately all human beings know that being enslaved is an unnatural and unjust experience. Enslaved people did not just passively accept their circumstances or the conditions in which they found themselves. We in the current generation may have mistakenly assumed that the enslaved were content with their lives but the literature and historical records give us a more accurate picture.

No matter how much they wished to, plantation owners could not control the thoughts, emotions, nor the aspirations of the enslaved. Some ways in which the enslaved resisted their circumstances ranged from the very subtle to more overt or aggressive actions.

Subtle actions of resistance may have included slow-walking the work, faking illness, or even refusing alcohol during holiday periods when slave owners encouraged the enslaved to become intoxicated. Cicely Lewis in her work *Resistance to Slavery* discusses these strategies used by enslaved people, either as an individual, instinctual response or maybe sometimes as a group response.

Even in the harsh environment of Mississippi, which was a state founded specifically and primarily for the cultivation of cotton to enrich a handful of landowners, enslaved people resisted. Some escalated forms of resistance included learning to read, holding secret meetings, and leaving the plantation without permission. In the book *My Brother Slaves* the author Sergio A. Lussana details how enslaved men passed on information to their fellowmen to keep each other informed. Information was sometimes gathered from overheard conversations between owners. Other times from stolen newspapers and other literature, or from tidbits gathered on neighboring farms. Because enslaved men were often drivers, delivery workers, or may have been hired out to work in towns or villages, they had greater access to the flow of information. In the slave narratives, William Webb, formerly enslaved in Mississippi, speaks of organizing a group of men to discuss options for possible escape in 1856. Webb talks about a secret meeting location where men would travel more than 10 miles from his farm and how they formed a patrol system for a lookout mechanism.

Eventually the courage, convictions, and resolve of men such as William Webb led to their fight for freedom which was sanctioned by the United States government. Before the Union won the Civil War, its military generals realized it needed more manpower, so began to actively recruit black enslaved men. Enslaved people left the plantations in large numbers when they saw how helping the Union might lead to freedom. They became active participants in achieving their own freedom, and did not simply wait to be set free.

By 1863 more than 17,000 black men in Mississippi enlisted in the Union Army fighting on the side of the North. They were classified as the United States Colored Troops and there were similar battalions throughout the South. In addition the families of these men, their wives, children, mothers, other relatives fled to Union Army camps where they assisted the military by cooking, cleaning, attending the wounded, and other tasks. Thereby large numbers of enslaved people in Mississippi took a risk to achieve their own freedom. Author Ann Murrell Taylor follows the actions of enslaved woman Eliza Bogan in the book *Embattled Freedom: Journeys Through the Civil War's Slave Refugee Camps* (2018) Eliza joined her husband at the Mississippi River Valley Union Army camp in the summer of 1863, showing extreme courage and resolve while escaping from her previous enslaver. While at the camp she also survived a military assault on the area by Confederate forces. Eliza's story is just one of the many examples of how enslaved people resisted their condition and fought for their own freedom.

Emancipation and Jubilee

Once slavery ended in the United States, following the Civil War, the formerly enslaved people had to make a life for themselves. In many instances there was a great deal of success, such as Greenwood, Oklahoma, known as Black Wall Street and Rosewood, Florida, among other towns. In Mississippi the primary example is the all-black town of Mound Bayou near the Tennessee border.

Mound Bayou, MS was established in 1887 by the formerly enslaved, and led by a man named Isaiah Montgomery. The town remains incorporated today and is listed on the National Register of Historic Places. One of its most prominent residents in the Civil Rights era was Dr Theodore Roosevelt Howard, known as T.R.M. Howard received his medical training in California at the institution which is currently Loma Linda University. Due to extreme discrimination and resentment from the white medical community of his leadership position in a Nashville, TN, hospital, Howard moved to Mound Bayou in 1942 where he became the chief surgeon for the local all-black hospital.

Through his diligence and ambition, Howard was able to help revitalize the community that suffered decline in the 1920's when the state confiscated black-owned lands through taxes and other nefarious means. In addition, he offered jobs to residents when he founded a hospital, insurance company, and a home construction firm. He raised cotton, cattle, quail, and hunting dogs on his 1000-acre farm. Howard provided medical services to the local black and some of the whites through his Friendship Clinic.

Howard became a leading advocate for voting rights and was a mentor to the budding civil rights activists in the area including Medgar Evers, Fannie Lou Hamer, Amzie Moore, and Aaron Henry, a future leader of the Mississippi Freedom Democratic Party.

Its hard to even imagine the loss to the Mound Bayou community which occurred when Dr Howard was forced to sell off his properties (at a great loss) and leave his home following the aftermath of the Emmett Till kidnapping, lynching and murder. In the trial of Till's alleged murderers, Roy Bryant and J. W. Milam, many civic minded leaders of the area collaborated to bring justice to the Till family. Dr Howard played a prominent role in the attempt to see justice served for such a blatant, horrendously bigoted, and inhumane act.

Because of his courageous efforts, Dr Howard suffered the consequences of extreme threats to himself and family. Simeon Booker, a reporter for the iconic Jet Magazine, who was in Sumner, MS in September, 1955 to cover the trial of Emmett Till's murderers was also given shelter, along with other black reporters on Dr Howard's estate. Booker states in his book *Shocking the Conscience* that following the acquittal of Bryant and Milam the local White Citizens Council placed a $1000 bounty on Dr Howard's life. Dr Howard reportedly said that he could "do more in the battle for Negro rights alive anywhere in the North than dead in a weed-grown grave in Dixie."[3]

What happened in Mound Bayou was directed at a specific individual in the case of Dr Howard, but is an excellent example of how once again white supremacy utilized terroristic strategies to interrupt, demoralize, and demolish the accomplishments of African American establishments.

Although Mound Bayou was a success story overall, many formerly enslaved people throughout the state of Mississippi were caught up in Black Code laws which strangled and stifled many aspects of their lives. Those laws along with racial customs reduced millions of Black people to sharecropping, a system designed to rob Black farmers of their labor and potential well-being and wealth. Sharecropping meant that a black farmer received all his supplies from a landowner, whose property he was "sharing". And at the end of the year the black farmer turned over all of his produce to the same landowner, his boss. This system might have actually worked if applied with fairness, but in the majority of cases, there was rampant abuse, fraud, and oppression. Many black farmers and their families remained in poverty because at the end of the year they always saw a deficit, they owed the white landowner and saw themselves in a cycle of perpetual debt.

In addition to sharecropping abuses, even when African-Americans owned land the state controlled how much of the property might be devoted to production of crops for marketing. In her autobiography *Coming of Age in Mississippi*, Ann Moody, renown Civil Rights activist from the 1960's speaks of how the farmers in Canton, Mississippi were restricted. She talked about how in 1963 the Black population of Canton exceeded the white population by more than two-thirds and the Blacks owned 40 percent of the land in the area. However, due to state laws and policies, black farmers were only allowed to grow marketable products such as cotton on a very small portion of their lands, therefore never being able to secure a profitable livelihood from farming.

In other areas of the state Black people were only allowed to rent land within city limits, and had little access to independent farming. It is then not surprising that at least two million African-Americans left the state of Mississippi, beginning in the 1920's up until the early 1970's, becoming part of the Great Migration.

Me and Papa at the Store

I was only ten years old, but I understood that there was a hierarchy in our world. It was a world of two societies. One black and one white. We lived in a totally segregated society in a small town on the Gulf Coast. Still living there came with a few 'bragging rights.' After all, my town had a beach, a pier with ships sailing in from other countries, we had streets of small shops like Woolworths, Sears, and JC Penney. But as a black child my world was very insulated, and we were restricted from certain activities such as using the main library or going to the beach. The 'separate but equal' library in my black neighborhood was a one-room addition to the small community recreation center. At the downtown movie theater, we had to sit in the balcony, though our tickets cost the same as those white kids sitting on the main floor. So mostly we went to the movies in our own neighborhood since we were fortunate enough to have a black-owned theater within walking distance. We called our theater "Miss Bama's" named for the wife of the owner, who also lived in our neighborhood.

We had very little contact with others outside of our race. Our home was in a segregated community, our school had all-black teachers, and church was certainly all-black. As young children we were not exposed so much to discrimination and racism as our parents and the community provided a shield and protection as best they could.

We rarely ventured out to areas where we might be unwanted. And our neighborhoods offered most services from local black businesses such as cab drivers, dry-cleaners, mom-and-pop convenience stores, a few restaurants, and nightclubs. There were street peddlers who sold fresh caught fish and crabs or other seafood. Others sold household products and sewing supplies from their trucks. So in the '50's and early 60's, our communities provided a natural buffer from racism for the children and youth to a certain extent. We had our own lives and the joy and love of family in our own black world. It would remain that way until I entered ninth grade, a young teenager being one of the first in the area, along with perhaps ten other black children, to attend a desegregated school.

When we would visit my grandmother in the summers, we called it "going to the country." But it was always fun because of all the cousins and relatives who were there. Everyone was friendly and always excited to see us. Plus, we could run and play in the pastures and race down to the creek. Going to town was another adventure. Newton County town had a two-block business district. I can remember a town square, maybe a bank, the sheriff's office and a few stores. It felt as if we black folks could only shop in a few places, mainly in the general store.

One hot summer day me and Papa walked the four or five miles on the dusty, red clay road to go to the store. I don't remember what we went to buy, maybe flour, cornmeal, or some other staple. It wasn't eggs or milk because my grandmother raised her own chickens and milk cows, and never had to shop for those items.

Anyway, when it was time to check out and pay for our purchases, my Papa was short by a small amount. Maybe for the sales tax? I'm not quite sure, but he was short by about twenty-five cents maybe. As he struggled to find *more coins in his pockets, the store clerk became impatient. I don't believe the clerk used a racial slur or anything, but I do recall the clerk's air of contempt, mainly through his facial expressions and body language. I was wondering why this person was angry with Papa. At the time I was holding a cracker jacks box, a very popular 1960's snack-treat consisting of caramel popcorn with nuts. My aunts, cousins and other relatives had given me a small stash of coins which I was saving and had thrown into the bottom of the snack box.*

Papa and I both felt the pressure of the moment, a feeling heading toward panic. Those were the days when a black person did not want to risk any incident that might annoy a white person. No matter how small the offense. Especially not in public.

I was able to shake out a quarter and maybe a few nickels and pennies to cover Papa's shortage. We never talked about it, but even as a child I could feel his quiet humiliation. I did not have the words to express how unjust and unfair the incident was. I had to keep those feelings to myself. Just one small moment of everyday life in Jim Crow America.

The state of Mississippi was determined to maintain the power structure of white dominance and supremacy. So they took strict measures to make sure that Black and indigenous people would remain second-class citizens. The state constitution was amended to severely repress the black vote way back in 1890. That action shaped Mississippi voting policies well into the mid-20th century. First a poll tax and a literacy test were imposed on the people. The law asked citizens who wanted to register to vote to provide a 'reasonable interpretation' of the state constitution. The wording of this law was intentionally vague. So on the surface it appeared the law was meant to be applied to all citizens, but in practice, these laws were strictly used against African-American voters. For example, in Canton, Mississippi in 1963, there were only 200 African-American registered voters, out of the 29,000 population of potential voters, according to Moody.

Essentially black Americans in the South and particularly those in Mississippi were prevented from voting up until the Voting Rights Act was passed by Congress in 1965.

In relation to legal struggles of African-Americans in the state, the conditions were totally stifling. When Black people were accused of wrong-doing and went before a judge in court, they were almost always facing an all-white jury and never a jury of their peers. This was a predictable outcome of a system which selected juries from the voter registration rolls, where most Black people were non-existent, having been denied the right to vote by state law and statutes.

However, by 1948 there was a case where an African-American plaintiff filed a lawsuit against the state of Mississippi protesting unequal pay for teachers' salaries. There had been a tradition of a huge discrepancy between white and Black salaries for teachers in the state, even though both groups were required to have the same qualifications for hiring. Black teachers were typically paid about half the salaries of white teachers. *Gladys Noel Bates v. The State of Mississippi: Equal Pay for Black Educators* was a landmark case that reportedly involved work by Thurgood Marshall. Bates' lawsuit was denied by local and state courts but not backing down, her case was eventually submitted to the US Supreme Court. However, the state of Mississippi settled with the plaintiffs before it was heard. Apparently, the state felt compelled to equalize the salaries of its teachers, although there were still horrific consequences for Gladys Bates. Bates and her husband, who also was a Jackson, MS Public Schools employee, was both fired from their jobs. Not only were they blacklisted in Mississippi but throughout the South, according to a report published in 2023 by Roslyn Anderson, WLBT-3 news, Jackson.

Bates and her family were forced to move to Colorado after surviving drive-by gunshots at their home and eventually the burning of their home to the ground by hostile assailants, who would be called "domestic terrorists" in today's language. In 2010 Gladys Bates died at the age of 90. Also that year, the Jackson Public Schools District finally honored Gladys Noel Bates by naming an elementary school after her.

Not only did teachers and other black professionals have to fight for fair wages, but many were systematically persecuted for any hint of political involvement. The state of Mississippi formed an agency called the Mississippi State Sovereignty Commission as a backlash measure against the US Supreme Court's *Brown vs. Board of Education* decision to outlaw segregation in the nation's schools in 1954. Mississippi was determined to protect its white supremacy climate at all costs and went on a rampage by targeting members of the NAACP and any others fighting against racial oppression. In his 2003 memoir *Ever is a Long Time*, W. Ralph Eubanks talks about when he discovered his parents had been on a list of names targeted by the Commission. His mother was a teacher and his father a county agricultural agent in Mount Olive, Mississippi in 1959. Eubanks is the former Director of Publishing of the Library of Congress in Washington, D.C., and decided to review the Mississippi Sovereignty Commission documents when the files were made public in 1998. Eubanks stated that "anything you did in Mississippi in the mid-1950s ....might land your name on a list of *suspicious* people to be watched." Furthermore, the Commission also funneled taxpayer dollars to the Citizens' Council, commonly known, according to Eubanks as the "uptown Klan."

The stigma of Mississippi's reputation is still being reconciled even today in the 21st century, however the healing of time is slowly evolving to produce a renewed environment where African-Americans may claim the rights of full citizenship. Black Mississippians like Black people throughout the nation have always made strides in education, industry, religion, and most importantly in caring for each other. Advances which have been made despite the obstacles.

But in order to achieve statewide and national reconciliation all the youth of this nation, all ethnicities, must be taught the accuracy of history. The old adage or saying is still true today as it has proven true down through the ages: "we have to know where we've been to know where we're going." We must learn from the past in order to plan for the future.

CHAPTER 2

Bright Horizon, Bright Tomorrows

After the tumultuous days of the Civil Rights Movement, the somewhat carefree days of the disco 1970s, and the Reagan-era War on Drugs of the 1980s, many Black people who had migrated to places like Chicago, St Louis, and Detroit or those who had gone out West began to miss the warmth, the ambience, and the new sense of potential back in their home states. As the South began to offer more opportunities and with some of the shackles of Jim Crow having been removed, going back home became more attractive to many.

Adding to this sentiment of longing for home was the growing decline and dysfunction in some major cities for many African-American neighborhoods and populations. Factories had begun to move overseas to take advantage of lower tax rates, so many jobs had been lost. The "War on Drugs" led to the Crime Bill of the 1990s which led to mass incarceration of millions of Black men across the nation. In far too many instances, Black families were broken and splintered.

So by the 1990s Reverse Migration was in full-swing for African-Americans all across this nation, with the state of Mississippi being one such destination. Our people began to come home, home to the beauty of rolling hills, red clay in some areas and blue-black rich soil in the Delta. They saw the Mississippi River, its power and beauty as it borders the length of the state to the west. They came back to the Gulf Coast and its well-kept secret white-sand beaches, palm trees, and beautiful Florida-like landscapes. They remembered the smell of biscuits piping hot from the oven or from woodstoves, sausages and roast beef, pound cakes and peach cobblers. All of the good smells of home. They remembered the hugs, the smiles, the eyes of welcome. Many had left families behind. So they came home. Even though Mississippi was a word that sometimes felt like a curse.

Despite all the history of oppression, all the difficulties, the restraints placed upon our humanity, Mississippi is still home, home to millions of Black people. So the Reverse Migration began, was real and people returned home.

Renaissance in Jackson

In the year 2013 a prominent community activist and civil rights attorney brought fresh energy and revitalization to the city of Jackson, Mississippi, which by then had a majority Black population. Chokwe Lumumba was born in Detroit to parents who had migrated there from Kansas and from Alabama. His family was active in their communities and encouraged their children's involvement as well. Chokwe was affiliated with the New Afrika Movement as a college student. He completed a law degree from Wayne

State University, Detroit in 1973. After having lived in Mississippi off and on during the seventies and eighties, he became a permanent resident in 1988, practicing law and serving several years on the Jackson City Council. In July 2013 he ran for mayor against the incumbent Harvey Johnson and won the election. Lumumba began to implement improvements right away by pushing a ballot initiative to add 1% to local sales taxes in order to fund badly needed infrastructure. Even though the state government officials tried to block his efforts, Lumumba succeeded in getting the initiative on the ballot, which was approved by the voters in January 2014. Unfortunately, Lumumba passed away only one month later in February 2014 while serving in the office of Mayor.

Jackson, Mississippi's gain was Lumumba's son, Chokwe Antar Lumumba who won the mayoral race in 2017. Lumumba, the son, born in 1983, had achieved his law degree from the Thurgood Marshall School of Law at Texas Southern University in 2008. He established his own firm in Jackson, MS by 2013 after working for his father's firm for a while. Chokwe Antar viewed himself as a progressive and allied himself with national political figures like Bernie Sanders and Nina Turner (Ohio).

The younger Lumumba served as mayor of Jackson for 8 years and was instrumental in saving the city zoo, in increasing arts and cultural activities, and providing more avenues for community involvement in government. The father-son Lumumba team proved to have a positive impact on the city of Jackson and thereby boosted the economy and outlook for the entire state of Mississippi.

In 2020 Mississippi received an added boost to its status and reputation in the person of PrimeTime super athlete, Deion Sanders, who accepted the position of head football coach at Jackson State University. The *Businessdownload.com* stated... "being one of the most media-savvy NFL legends comes with a lot of influence. {Deion} Sanders brought the media flair with him when he arrived in Jackson...."[4]

Shortly after Sanders arrived as head coach, the stadium sold out bringing more than 60,000 attendees to a game against Jackson State's top rival, Alcorn State. Soon, Jackson State was able to recruit top athletes like Travis Hunter and Deion's son Shedeur Sanders.

Not stopping there, Deion Sanders was instrumental in securing a media rights deal for Jackson State's football association, the Southwestern Athletic Conference (SWAC). This was a gigantic success and achievement for SWAC leading to greater financial resources and national exposure.

And perhaps most promising of all is that Sanders or Coach Prime, started a movement among African-American coaches and sportsmen. Even though his later move to the University of Colorado was controversial, his time at Jackson State inspired both players and coaches to take a closer look at HBCUs to utilize their talents. Now there is Michael Vick at Norfolk State in Virginia and Eddie Robinson, Jr at Alabama State University. Other former NFL players like Samie Parker, Terence Garvin, and Elton Brown have coaching assistant roles at Delaware State University and Norfolk State, respectively.

This evolution among elite athletes toward embracing HBCU sports programs provides inspiration to an entire generation of young people to build up their own institutions and communities.

All of these developments point toward African-Americans returning to the South, reclaiming our roots and working toward brighter futures for our children and grandchildren and for future generations to come.

Political Success among Black Candidates

Currently in 2025, a quarter-century into the new millennium, there is hope on the horizon for states like Mississippi, and generally for the South. Slowly but steadily the African-American population has achieved milestones since the Civil Rights Movement of the late 1960s. Education was always a key value among the Black population. Even during slavery there were countless examples of enslaved people risking their lives to learn how to read. After Emancipation history shows us how Black people started schools in homes and churches, despite having very limited resources. Education was one of the top priorities of our newly freed ancestors. Once discrimination was outlawed or at least 'politically incorrect' in some cases, our people made strides towards college education, professional and/ or vocational training, and job acquisition. Today African-Americans make up a huge percentage of college graduates in this nation.

In the realm of political activism, currently there are several grassroots organizations which are fighting tirelessly to register, promote, and to educate communities about the power of voting. The organization Mississippi Votes headed by Arekia Bennett offers voter outreach, youth mobilization and other strategies to increase voter participation among Black voters in the state.

In addition Latosha Brown is the co-founder of Black Voters Matter and is a nationally recognized advocate for voters' rights. She has worked tirelessly for decades to increase voter turnout and to fight voter suppression throughout the country, but in particular in the South, including within the state of Mississippi.

The activism of some national figures is helping to increase political awareness in the state as well. Stacy Abrams, who coincidentally spent some of her formative years in Mississippi. Abrams, who is a brilliant voter registration strategist, founded the Fair Fight Organization, which specializes in voter suppression litigation. Abrams is currently supporting a Mississippi candidate for US Senate, Scott Colom.

Of course, Abrams became a household name when she ran for governor of the state of Georgia both in 2018 and 2022. She has been candid in critiquing the Democratic Party leadership for not devoting more resources and attention to Mississippi and other Southern states, where the

African-American population is approximately 40% of the state and potentially a source of increased voting power for the Democratic Party. Abrams has also rightfully called out the party in its relative neglect of Black voters in the entire Southern region.

Despite the national political climate of 2025, which has leanings toward a far-right and White Nationalist agenda, there are numerous, bright political spots in Mississippi. Several state representative positions, judgeships, local councils and other political positions are being filled by African-American candidates.

In the run for the US Senate seat which will be held in 2026, there are two other African-American candidates besides Colom. Colom will face Priscilla Williams-Till, a relative of the iconic martyr Emmett Till in the Democratic Primary prior to the Senate election. And another more seasoned politician Ty Pinkins is running as an independent. Pinkins is an attorney and a U.S. Army veteran.

Mississippi is poised today to witness sweeping changes in the landscape of opportunities for its Black citizens. Politically there are more African-Americans who hold public offices or who are competing for public offices. In fact, the results of the Special Election held in November 2025 are extremely encouraging for the state. Two African-American candidates were elected to the state Senate, and one additional candidate flipped a Republican-held state house seat.

The home ownership among African-Americans has risen to 53%, which is a big improvement even though lagging behind the average for the entire state, which is at 69%. Land ownership for agriculture among African-Americans remains low, however, those challenges are being studied and supported by the work of organizations like the Black Farmers Alliance. Overall income levels for African-Americans have also increased over the past few decades.

The state's economy has received a boost over the past few decades through its tourism. The Mississippi Gulf Coast is naturally beautiful, bordering the Gulf of Mexico and had been a quiet haven for the affluent as a vacation spot since the 1920s. But in modern times there has been a growing awareness that Mississippi offers white-sand beaches, casinos, a robust hotel industry, a new aquarium, and other attractions only 45 minutes away from New Orleans.

In its totality, the future for African-Americans looks bright in the state of Mississippi. More people are attending college or being trained for vocations or professional positions. With an increasing level of home ownership, increased incomes, and increased participation in the political process there is certainly a hopeful and bright future ahead for Mississippi's youth.

CHAPTER 3

The Story of Harriette Mapp

"The caged bird sings with a fearful trill, of things unknown, but longed for still, and his tune is heard on the distant hill, for the caged bird sings of freedom."

—Maya Angelou, I Know Why the Caged Bird Sings

I grew up knowing very little about my second great-grandmother. That feels a little shocking to realize and to admit. After all she was only one generation removed from my mother's grandparents, about whom I did hear some stories.

Harriette Mapp was born somewhere between 1825 and 1830, most likely in Georgia, according to the 1900 U.S. Census and the death certificates of two of her sons. Over time, we've seen her use several surnames—Mapp, Huddleston, and Williams. Interestingly, these names also appear among three white slaveholders who migrated from Georgia to Mississippi in the late 1850s. Based on census clues and DNA evidence, Harriette's deeper roots may trace back even further—to North Carolina or Virginia.

Dr. Elizabeth West explains in her book Finding Francis that many enslaved people did not know where their parents were born, due to the constant trafficking of human beings. By the early 1800s enslaved families were routinely separated and sold apart for profit, to satisfy debt, or during probate court (following the reading of a will). Or many enslaved people were sold on a whim or for revenge. So it's entirely possible Harriette was born in South Carolina, then moved to Georgia as a child, and eventually forced into Mississippi.

She may have been separated from her mother very early, much like Frederick Douglass was. In his 1845 classic Narrative of the Life, Douglass recalls being separated from his mother as a toddler. His enslaved mother worked miles away from her children and died when Frederick was still a young boy. Douglass grew up on a Maryland plantation that enslaved over a thousand people—just imagine that scale, where human beings were ruthlessly sent to harvest tobacco, wheat, or corn. Children were often left behind in the care of elderly women no longer able to work the fields.

Harriette may have faced a similar fate: removed from her parents, unsure of where they were sent, if they were sold, or if she'd ever see them again.

This was the world Harriette entered—a world she would endure until the Emancipation Proclamation, and beyond. There's some evidence that she was enslaved by a white family who relocated from Georgia to Mississippi in the 1850s. If she traveled with them rather than being sold at auction, that might have offered the minor advantage of familiarity, if nothing else.

We're still piecing together the exact nature of Harriette's connection to the white Mapp and Huddleston families, both of whom were considered deeply religious and highly educated for their time. These families founded churches and schools in several Southern states. Their ranks included lawyers and teachers—an elite class among white Southerners. But their religious beliefs did not prevent them from being a part of the market economy of that time. They owned human beings and chose to make their livelihood and profit from the enslavement of African descendants.

During the early 1800s, Southern planters from Virginia and North Carolina began moving westward, looking for new land after exhausting the soil in their home states. Once the U.S. government forcibly removed the Cherokee and Choctaw from their ancestral lands, white settlers quickly moved in and were sold property at bargain prices. One such family, the Taliaferros—chronicled in Wright Thompson's The Barn—epitomized this migration. They moved from Virginia into South Carolina, then Georgia, and eventually Mississippi, building large cotton plantations along the way. We have a theory that my enslaved ancestor Harriette Mapp may have been brought to Mississippi under similar circumstances.

By the end of the Civil War, Harriette was living in Newton County, Mississippi. The 14th Amendment had finally granted citizenship to the formerly enslaved African-Americans. But we don't know how she felt about her forced relocation—did she ever long to return to Georgia or North Carolina? Did she have family back there she never saw again? Or did she eventually come to embrace her new home? It's hard to say. We were unable to find records of her parents or any siblings.

Although we could not locate Harriette in the 1870 census, the 1880 records tell us that over her lifetime, she had given birth to eleven children, with nine surviving. Initially we were only able to identify six of those children. Her first two children were born in Georgia; the rest, in

Mississippi. That timeline alone tells a story. It indicates that my great-great grandmother had no choice about leaving Georgia and coming to Mississippi. It shows that she was probably uprooted from her family, that she had to leave behind her parents and possibly her sisters and brothers. Even if her parents were deceased at the time she left, she may have been closer to other family members back there. Essentially Harriette had been torn away from her home and the roots of family.

But Harriette was able to push through and made the best of her circumstances. Through local church records, we discovered that Harriette was a founder and board member of Spring Hill Baptist Church—one of Newton County's earliest Black churches. Her name appears alongside John Huddleston, a respected businessman and the church's first pastor. Other founding members included Richard "Dick" Mapp and several members of the Cleveland family. The Clevelands become central to our family story, too, through later intermarriage with two of Harriette's sons.

At some point before or after emancipation, Harriette lived with or married Richard "Dick" Mapp, who was a community leader. Though we haven't located a marriage certificate, there's good reason to believe Dick Mapp was Harriette's husband or long-term partner, and the father of several of her children. Richard Mapp has also been identified as "Bill" Mapp according to oral history, but no records have been found to substantiate the name "Bill". Otherwise, there is a listing on Coleman Mapp's death certificate which states that Coleman's father is Richard W. Mapp. This has been interpreted by some family members to mean that 'William' is a middle name, and "Bill" is the nickname.

We found a Freedmen's Bureau document where Dick Mapp filed a labor complaint. We also found a Dick Mapp on the Newton County, Mississippi voter roll in 1867. Richard "Dick" Mapp, my apparent second great grandfather, may have been a community activist based upon what scant information we do have. By 1880, he disappeared from the record, and Harriette is listed as a widow. His disappearance naturally leads to speculation about his whereabouts during that time. Maybe something nefarious happened to him, given the documented history and climate of lynching after Reconstruction. We have few clues to determine what may have happened to Dick Mapp, finding no death records and no family stories which had been passed down.

Not being able to find Harriette or her children in the 1870 census has been frustrating. A few things might explain the gap. She may have changed her name after emancipation—something many formerly enslaved people did to establish a new identity. Or perhaps she was living in another household under a different name, such as rooming as a tenant with others, or working as a servant to former slaveholders and living in servants quarters. It's also possible that her children were held by former enslavers as unpaid laborers, a cruel but common practice in the postwar South. Then again, maybe the census taker simply missed them. We believe Harriette was in Mississippi at that time—there's no evidence to show that she returned to Georgia or relocated elsewhere—but we're still searching for this key piece of her puzzle.

Sometime in the 1870s, less than ten years after Emancipation, Harriette became a landowner. She held deeds for 80 acres of land in Newton County. In 1882, she co-owned some of this land with Frank Walton. Initially we believed that Frank was only a family friend or a neighbor. Later research showed that Frank was actually Harriette's son-in-law. His wife—Roxanna or "Roxie" Mapp Walton—we later confirmed through DNA analysis to be Harriette's daughter. That connection helped explain the strong bond between the Mapp and Walton families during the 1880s into the 1900s.

However, by 1910, Frank and Roxanna were no longer married. By 1920 many of the couple's children had left the state and migrated to Texas. Roxanna may have died in the state of Texas. We found one source which

35

shows that Roxie may have resided in Nacogdoches, Texas with her son Frank Robert Walton at the time of her death in 1941. It appears that Roxie's descendants have scattered throughout the West, and unfortunately their ties to the family in Newton County appear to have been broken.

In 1885–86, Harriette is listed as guardian for four children who appear on state school rolls, though not on the federal census as living in her household. We were thrilled to later confirm they were her grandchildren, likely left in her care after the death or disappearance of their mother, Ann Huddleston. We last see Ann in the 1870 census, raising six children: Sarah, Mollie, Charles, William, Harriette, and Emma. Sadly, because Mississippi did not require death certificates until 1912, we haven't been able to learn what happened to Ann, Harriette's oldest known daughter. There is scant information to trace the whereabouts of Ann's six children, which would be an interesting project for future family historians.

As stated, Harriette initially co-owned farmland with Frank Walton but by 1885, her son John Mapp was listed as a co-owner. In 1886, Harriette was the sole landholder of her property. That means that in her late 50s or early 60s, Harriette was not only holding her own—she was thriving, at least for a few years. In 1890 she owned two plots of land, which equaled 160 acres. The market value at that time would have been over one thousand dollars, roughly forty thousand dollars in today's buying power.

It is unfortunate that Harriette was forced to sell the land in December 1890 for far less than market value. She received approximately $350.00 for the sale. We were not able to determine the circumstances but it's likely that the land was mortgaged and perhaps the family struggled to make lien payments. The sale is documented by the Newton County Chancery Court Deed Book, accessed via FamilySearch.org.

Harriette helped establish Spring Hill Baptist Church in 1866, alongside Dick Mapp and others. Pastor John Huddleston, who donated the initial land for the church building, may have been Harriette's relative.

DNA suggests a link between the two, though we haven't confirmed the exact relationship. Harriette left behind a remarkable legacy which included building a church community, raising children, and managing her land. Her story is very fascinating, especially since we knew so little about her prior to our family history search.

Thanks to modern tools like AncestryDNA, we've since identified hundreds of previously unknown cousins. A handful I knew already through family stories shared by my mother and grandmother. But most like the Waltons, were new to me. Even so they are part of Harriette's legacy, too. She endured extraordinary hardship and yet left behind something precious and enduring: a family that stretches across generations and continues to grow.

CHAPTER 4

The Six Sons of Harriette

Charlie Mapp

My great-grandfather Charlie Mapp was born around 1860 in Newton County and was Harriette's third son. According to the 1880 US Census he lived with his mother and other siblings and they farmed the land for a living. He was nineteen or twenty years old at that time and helped his mother, who was a widow. He would have mastered the chores of farming by that age such as caring for animals, plowing, weeding, planting and harvesting crops.

Charlie married my great-grandmother Mary Jefferson in 1894, when she was about sixteen years of age. They eventually had a total of ten children together. Their second child Larcenia was my grandmother.

Mary and Charlie were married for over thirty years until his death in the early 1920s. The 1920 US Census shows that he was living with Mary and their eight children at that time. Their oldest child and daughter, Leola, was married and had her own household by 1920.

Charlie was a farmer who owned land in 1910 but by 1920 the family resided in a rental property again, according to the records.

We have very few documents which trace Charlie's lifespan in Newton County. Since he was born during the Civil War era, we were not expecting to find much, but hoped for perhaps Bible records. Despite the fact that Mississippi began to require death records in 1912, we could not locate a death certificate after a diligent search.

One interesting documented fact we uncovered was that Charlie had married Gracie Cleveland in 1887, before marrying my great-grandmother Mary Jefferson in 1894. We have a record of the marriage license for both marriages. No children are known from his first marriage, nor has any oral history been passed down about Gracie. So their marriage remains a mystery in some respects. We can only surmise that since Gracie and Frances Cleveland were sisters, that Charlie and his brother Coleman married a sister duo.

We do have some limited oral history accounts of Charlie's life which have been passed down by our relatives. But since my mother was born after Charlie's death she was unable to pass down any firsthand stories about him to her own children.

One key to understanding Charlie's final years came from my late brother Rick, who had a very good rapport with family elders. Among Rick's papers, we found notes from a conversation he previously had with our great-aunt Eloise. Eloise was one of the youngest among Charlie's daughters.

Aunt Eloise recalled being around eight years old when her father became gravely ill. One day while bedridden he asked her to bring him a drink of water, but by the time she returned with the glass of water he was unresponsive. Sadly her father had passed away quietly in bed.

My aunt's conversation with my brother Rick helped to solve a mystery for me, because it confirmed that my great-grandfather Charlie had likely died of natural causes. Previously because there was so little known information passed on about him, and because we could not locate a death record, I had imagined the worst, that perhaps Charlie had met a nefarious ending. And especially given the time of Jim Crow terror through which he would have lived. It was a relief to discover that was not the case and that Charlie died at home surrounded by family.

Coleman Mapp

Coleman was born around 1863 and follows my great-grandfather in birth order among Harriette's children. He was apparently an industrious young man who, like his older brothers, was living with their mother in 1880 helping her provide for the family.

A marriage certificate dated July, 1884 verifies that Coleman was wed to Frances Cleveland. He would have been twenty-one years old and she was around sixteen at that time. The couple would eventually have a total of eleven children.

Coleman was an educator and active community leader during his day. In the early 1920s he founded Pilgrim Rest Baptist Church and became the church's first pastor. Pilgrim Rest as an institution remains viable today in 2025, and is very much loved and revered by the network of Mapp family relatives and by the community at large. Before establishing the church Coleman was instrumental in starting a school for Black children of Newton County during the time period prior to state funded education.

COLEMAN MAPP. *Son of Harriette Huddleston MAPP and Richard W. "Bill" MAPP. Image of wall plaque at Pilgrim Rest Baptist Church, Decatur MS. From collection of Bobby Mapp.*

An account of Coleman's life was provided by his youngest daughter, Flossie Mapp Thornton in a family reunion booklet prepared by his descendants in 1978. Flossie passed on an oral account from her memories of her father's community and civic activities. He was the chairperson of the Long Pilgrim Association, which sought to improve the lives of his parishioners.

Coleman left a legacy of being a hard worker, a landowner and being an accomplished businessman of the era. Also he displayed courage and determination during a time when it was expected that African-Americans would accept the status quo and not seek fair treatment. Coleman filed a grievance in the courts.

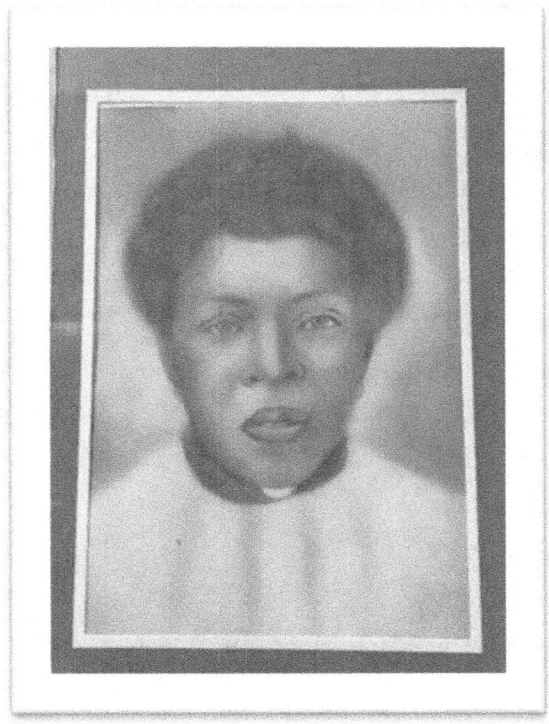

Frances Cleveland MAPP, *wife of Coleman, mother of ten of his children. Preceded him in death in 1923. Image of wall plaque at Pilgrim Rest Baptist Church, Decatur MS. From collection of Bobby Mapp.*

Frances Mapp, Coleman's wife and mother of ten of his children died in 1923. Eventually as a widower, Coleman married Stella Miller in 1927. Census records show no indication that any children were born to Coleman and Stella's union.

Coleman died at the venerable age of 89 shortly after the 1950 Census was taken, a document on which he appears as living with his wife Stella. His death record indicates that he passed away on April 20, 1950, leaving a legacy of dedication, commitment, and love for his family and community.

Prince Mapp

Prince Mapp appears to be Harriette's oldest son. He was born in 1857 or 1858 and was living in the home with his mother and four other brothers in 1880. He was twenty-two years old at the time according to the 1880 US Census records.

Prince married Sarah "Sallie" Dallas in 1881. They had three known children together, two daughters, Velma and Georgia, and one son, Green. Documents also indicate that Prince fathered several other children in addition to those born to his wife Sarah, but we were unable to confirm the identities of the mothers.

Prince's oldest daughter Velma married Joseph Wilson, who was employed by the State Department of Agriculture. The Wilsons were considered affluent members of the county and were community leaders.

Though Prince is apparently Harriette's oldest son, I had never heard family members speak of him directly. But Prince's daughter Velma and her husband live vividly in my childhood memory as Cousin Velma and Cousin Joseph. I must have seen them half a dozen times when I was growing up, usually during the summer visits with my grandmother.

Cousin Velma's house seemed special to me as a little kid—a big white house on a hill with a wraparound porch, so different from the smaller unpainted tin-roofed houses that many of my other relatives lived in.

Velma's husband drove a pickup truck, not a mule-drawn wagon like my grandmother and her neighbors. In the early 1960s, only a few African Americans in Newton County owned cars.

As a child, it felt as if everyone I met in that small community was called cousin, aunt or uncle. Only years later did I understand that Velma was indeed my grandmother's biological first cousin, and that Prince was my mother's blood uncle. The 1910 U.S. Census even shows Harriette, at age

82, living with Prince and his family. So it appears that at the end of her life, Harriette spent her final days with Prince and his family.

In 1910 Prince was a farmer and landowner according to the US Census for that year. His wife Sarah died in 1914 and a few years later his son Green migrated to Flint, Michigan for better career opportunities. It was quite amazing to find that even though Prince was well past middle age in 1920, he moved to Louisiana to work in the paper mills in Bogalusa. According to the 1920 Federal Census Prince boarded with another Mississippian, Cleve Harris. They both, along with others in the household were listed as laborers in the paper mill. Historical accounts show that the Great Southern Lumber Company, owned by the world renowned Goodyear family, established a massive lumber operation in the southeastern Louisiana area beginning in 1914. By 1920 Bogalusa, LA was a prosperous lumber and sawmill town, from which Prince was apparently able to benefit.

By 1930 at the age of 75 Prince had returned to Mississippi and was listed as a single landowner. More research may reveal whether Prince ever re-married following the death of Sarah who had passed away so many years earlier.

In 1940 Prince was 90 years old and lived with his daughter Velma and her husband. Prince died at the age of 91 in 1941 in Newton County, where his internment was at Spring Hill Missionary Baptist Church Cemetery.

John, Benjamin, and George Mapp

Besides Prince, there were three other sons of Harriette who were scarcely mentioned, if at all, in my family circle: John, Benjamin or Ben, and George.

John was the most familiar to me because I remember my grandmother would sometimes mention him. I vaguely remember that his land was near my grandmother's place. He had two daughters, Belle and Vallie, who lived in Newton County into the 1980s. We never met them, but I vaguely knew they were "family." Later I learned that they were, in fact, my grandmother's first cousins.

Research shows that Belle and Vallie's descendants still live throughout Mississippi and beyond. I was even able to speak with some of Belle's descendants, though they knew few details about John's life, and we were unable to find his death certificate.

The two youngest sons, Benjamin and George, were complete mysteries and totally unknown to me until we began this genealogy journey.

Ben migrated to Flint, Michigan in the 1920s or 1930s, where he died in 1934 of heart failure. Records show he was an autoworker, and his death certificate confirms his parents were Harriette Williams (Mapp) and Richard Mapp. Ben's migration to Michigan will be featured in a later chapter of this book. George spent his entire life in Newton County where he lived to be 90 years old, dying of natural causes in 1954. George's daughter, Ora, was listed as the informant on his death certificate. Beyond that, little is known about George's life or about his descendants.

CHAPTER 5

The Family Matriarchs: Lionesses of Newton County

Mary Jefferson

Mary Jefferson, my great-grandmother, died when my mother was a little girl. But my mother always spoke of her and handed down stories about Mary. At some point in my youth I became fascinated by her name—it sounded distinguished and patriotic or like someone with authority.

Mary married my great-grandfather Charlie at a very young age, around age sixteen. In the 1910 Census the family included six children and increased to eight children by 1920.

Mary and Charlie had ten children together before his death in 1923. She had to carry the burdens of sharecropper life as a widow.

My mother would tell us how Mary would sit on the bank of a pond or a creek and fish for hours, sometimes with her sister. Mary's sister was known throughout the county as an herbalist and healer. My mother also sometimes went with her Aunt, the healer, to forage and look for herbs and medicinal plants or berries.

Mary Jefferson was a remarkable woman who also raised orphaned grandchildren after the deaths of her two eldest daughters. I'm so inspired by and admire Mary's life of dedication to her family. She showed resilience and courage despite her circumstances. One example is how my own mother spent a good portion of her childhood with her first cousins who were being raised by their grandmother Mary. They became like her siblings and were a big part of my mother's life. Their personalities, likes and dislikes, skills, and strengths were magnified by my mother's stories about them. So for me they were larger-than-life figures and it felt as if I knew them as well as my mother knew them.

Unfortunately for every family in the environment of the Jim Crow South, there existed a constant threat of white supremacy violence. My mother spoke of one cousin who was forced to sneak away in the middle of the night and leave the state to avoid being harassed or worse because he had a dispute with his white boss. It is hard to imagine in today's society that a worker might be jailed or worse for expressing a grievance about the job to his employer. But for African-Americans this was a common experience in the days of state-sanctioned racial discrimination.

Mary's love for family was reflected in her daily acts of care, faith, and perseverance. Her strong faith in a Higher Power, Almighty God was the key to her family's survival through extremely challenging times. She passed down a legacy of family members supporting and taking care of each other. Even though her and Charlie's descendants would scatter across the United

States during the Great Migration, the family remained tight-knit, loving and loyal to each other. These traits can be traced back directly to the leadership and examples set by our primary matriarch, Mary Jefferson.

LARCENIA MAPP WHITFIELD *lived in Newton County MS until her death in 1963. Was mother of one child, Margie Ree Amos and grandmother of thirteen. (From collection of Aishah Cowan)*

Larcenia "Larcine" Mapp Whitfield- A Life of Quiet Strength

Larcenia Mapp was born in 1899 according to the US Census Record for 1900. She is the second child born to Mary Jefferson and Charlie Mapp. Larcine gave birth to my mother in 1925. Larcine had married briefly and divorced twice before her final marriage to William "Sonny" Whitfield in 1948. She lived all of her life in Newton County Mississippi where she became a pillar of the community.

Although several of Charlie and Mary's children left the South and migrated to Chicago, Detroit, or California, my grandmother Larcine chose to remain in Newton County. She worked very hard every day, and in my memories of her I always visualize the land, her milk cows and chickens, and her daily chores.

When I visited my grandmother in the summers, the entire household would get out of bed very early every morning. Not only did she need to milk the cows, but she would also drive them down to the pasture, where they fed on the grass during the day. That may have been a half-mile walk from the house, there and back. My brother, Jimmy, and I would tag along with her following her yelping dog, whose job was to herd the cows.

And that was just for starters; my grandmother's day was just beginning. We would have to draw water from the well, which was midway between her house and the next farmhouse, about a quarter mile up the road, a steep incline walk.

Next the 10-gallon milk cans would be pushed out by the side of the road in front of the house to be picked up by the milkman. My grandmother earned extra income by selling cow's milk to the local dairy distribution company. By the time we kids cleaned up for breakfast she would have made biscuits from scratch. And to top that off, we had fresh butter from the churn and her peach or blackberry preserves, which she canned herself the previous fall maybe. We kind of took it for granted, but a breakfast like hers is not easy to come by in today's fast-paced world.

There is really no comparison to my grandmother's cooking. I can remember even at five or six years old I loved her green beans and squash. It was because my grandmother had cooked them. She would use a big cast-iron skillet, sauteeing them in a little oil, using a healthy sprinkling of black pepper and salt. Just fresh beans and squash from the garden. The aromas and tastes which came from her kitchen have a special place in my heart and spirit, and are part of her legacy, that which keeps her memory alive within me and my siblings.

I didn't realize it at the time, but my grandmother was a sort of free-lance field worker. She would take day-work at various locations around town to make ends meet. She might be in a corn field or soybean field for a few days, then she might 'chop cotton' on another farm the next week. By the time I was about ten, she began to plant her own patch of cotton, which she taught my brother and me to pick. Her area of the state had never been dedicated to the cultivation of cotton like in the Mississippi Delta. But cotton was grown in central Mississippi also and considered a lucrative crop.

I can remember feeling a little uncomfortable, having some feelings of shame being in that field and filling a sack up with cotton, as a ten-year-old. Even though the proceeds belonged to my grandmother and she was able to sell her harvest to the local cotton gin, there was still this sense of *'do we really have to do this? Isn't picking cotton slave work?'*

But my grandmother still made the whole outing fun because she would give us kids a treat, like extra peppermint or maybe nickels and dimes to spend on candy and gum at the town square. It was fun even though going to town on Saturday meant a three to four-mile walk in the hot sun. Usually we walked to town with Papa, my mother's stepfather, or with some of the older cousins. Papa walked with a limp but his condition did not slow him down and he made the walk to town without complaint.

Grandmother was usually too busy for those shopping trips, but she always made sure we prepared for Sunday. Going to church on Sundays was the highlight of our week. We would dress-up, ironing ribbons for my hair and Jimmy shining his black church shoes. For my grandmother it meant pulling down her good hat from the top of the closet. We had to look our very best because that was *the* special day for the entire community.

We would usually walk, which was also maybe a mile in the opposite direction from the cow pastures. Sometimes a neighbor or relative would give us a ride. But so few people owned cars in that community during those days that a ride was usually by mule-drawn wagon.

The Singing Contest

Everybody in town loved the glorious singing at Pilgrim Rest Church. Besides the sermon, the choir was the main attraction of Sunday morning service. "Amazing Grace", "Jordan River" and "Wade in the Water" seemed to be the most popular songs and my favorite ones. So my brother Jimmy and I knew those songs back and forth just like all the other kids who attended church with their parents, grandparents or aunties. At my grandmother's house We would all gather around the kitchen table or in the front room after supper and just talk or spend some time unwinding before bed and relaxing after a long day of chores. Because there was no TV or board games, we would sometimes have a singing contest. One night we decided to go head-to-head and sing the same song. I went first. I finished and sat down, feeling a little proud of myself.

"Jordan River, Jesus help me to cross," Jimmy started out in his smooth baritone voice. His head held high and his eyes gazing toward the ceiling he sang his heart out with emotions coming from his chest. When he finished, Grandmother and Papa congratulated him, clapped loudly and told him he would have a singing career one day.

My voice had sounded sort of like a chipmunk when I took my turn. My Papa was looking at me with a little bit of pity, like he wanted to say "bless her heart." But my grandmother knew exactly how to make me feel better after I lost the contest. She hugged me and told me that I should just keep on singing and one day I would be able to sing in the choir.

⚜ ⚜ ⚜

My brother Jimmy, at age 11 or 12. Me at age 9 or 10
(Photos from collection of Will Amos II)

Beyond regular church Sunday, there was the church anniversary, the epitome of worship and celebration.

Grandmother would prepare boxes of food to be shared with the entire congregation, sort of like a potluck dinner. The ladies would spread the food out on tables under the shade trees and serve the membership and visitors. People would sometimes travel back to town from the big cities where they may have migrated for these special "homecomings".

These potluck dinners were always delicious, with roast beef, fried chicken, fish, cornbread, collard greens, chicken and dumplings, fried or boiled corn, and a host of other vegetables straight from the gardens or the fields. And all the ladies seemed to be competing, and wanted bragging rights for the best fried chicken or best chocolate cake.

Desserts especially the beautiful, tasty cakes were always my favorites: coconut, chocolate, and pound cakes. Church anniversary 'Homecoming' was the day to fill up on all the treats.

The Loss of My Grandmother

In 1963, the summer right before my twelfth birthday, my family and I traveled to Newton County for my Grandmother's funeral. We were all heartbroken. It was the first time I had ever seen my mother express such grief, and on top of that, she had just given birth to twins, a baby boy and girl, two weeks earlier.

Some of the customs surrounding her death were bewildering to my twelve-year-old self.

First, by the time my parents arrived at my grandmother's house, her belongings were gone—claimed by neighbors or maybe distant relatives. There were no chairs left to sit on. Only a small bundle of her clothing, a few letters, and some photographs had been set aside for my mother. I remember my mother breaking down again when she realized how few mementos or keepsakes were left of her mother's earthly life. I felt so helpless, bewildered, and a little betrayed by the community. Why did they take all my grandmother's things? As I grew older I came to realize that that was just the local custom of the times, an expression of the community's love for my grandmother and what she had meant to them.

And I felt so sad that even though I often wrote letters to my grandmother, I did not have a chance to hear her voice over the year's time when she was battling cancer. Neither she nor my parents had a telephone in the home at that time.

Secondly, the night before the funeral, our grandmother's body was brought to the house for a wake. The small, four-room home was packed with mourners, with more people standing in the yard. I remember feeling overwhelmed and alone, watching the adults grieve and not knowing how to process my own sadness.

The funeral itself was a blur of songs, prayers, and ceremony, followed by the graveside service. Later, at the church repast, the mood lifted as relatives from up North and across the South reconnected, laughed, and told stories.

Even as a child, I carried the lesson of her life: quiet strength, daily sacrifice, and love for family. My grandmother, the granddaughter of Harriette, embodied resilience and grace.

As an adult I realize and feel very blessed to have had a grandmother who was a wonderful role model. She showed us, not so much in words but in her actions and her deeds, the power of hard work, and dedication to her family and community. She was the steady member of her family who others leaned on when times were hard. I witnessed my grandmother listen to her siblings, relatives or neighbors, offering them advice or just to show that she cared. My grandmother's quiet strength and steadfastness, her sense of purpose has helped guide me over the years. My prayer is that I will in turn be able to instill a fraction of her sense of character into my own grandchildren.

Matriarchs Cont'd: AUNT ELOISE

My great aunt Eloise Mapp Sims was a strong, loving personality, larger-than-life and had become one of the matriarchs of the extended family by the time I was in elementary school. She and her husband and children had relocated from Newton County to our town at some point during the late fifties or the early sixties. She was affectionately called "Mom-mee" by her biological grandchildren and by many other children in the neighborhood. Charlie had seven daughters and Aunt Eloise was one of the youngest ones. By the late 50's there were only four surviving daughters so I only got to meet those four in the flesh. Then in 1963 at the time of my grandmother's death, Aunt Eloise took on that role of becoming our grandmother in spirit.

Eloise Mapp Sims. *Daughter of Charlie and Mary Mapp, mother of five sons and one daughter, host of grandchildren and descendants. Lived on MS Gulf Coast until her death in 2007. Photo from the collection of Wilbur Sims.*

I remember Auntie telling us kids ghost stories. Her ghosts lived in the forest or the 'woods' and she called them "haints", shadowy figures who might help a person find buried pots of gold. The 'haints" also might, depending on their mood, cause all kinds of mayhem and send a man screaming and running for his life. We kids hung onto Auntie's every word of these stories. She was also the role model for being smart, clever, bold and outspoken and to top it off, she was one of the best-dressed ladies in church. Over the years Aunt Eloise became more and more precious and was a great resource for our extended family on the Gulf Coast. She almost lived to the century-mark, being 98 years old at the time of her death in 2007.

GLOVER SIMS, *husband of Eloise MAPP Sims, with whom he shared five sons and one daughter. Lived on Gulf Coast until death in 1974. Photo from the collection of Wilbur Sims.*

RACHEL SIMS MALONE *daughter of Eloise MAPP Sims. Photo from the collection of Al Malone.*

WOODROW SIMS, *son of Eloise MAPP Sims. Photo from the collection of Wilbur Sims*

WOODROW and **WILBERT SIMS**. *Sons of Eloise MAPP Sims. 1950's. Photo from the collection of Lucia Sims.*

WILL LEE SIMS (1950 - 2005), *son of Eloise MAPP Sims. Photo from the collection of Wilbur Sims*

Matriarch: Ella Mapp Reese

At the time that I met Ella Reese, I had no idea that she was my grandmother Larcine's first cousin. I was a ten-year-old and all I knew was that she was our cousin, like so many other people I spent time with in Newton County. Later in life I learned that Ella Reese was the daughter and third child of Coleman Mapp and his wife Frances. Ella was born in 1890 according to the 1900 US Census. By the time I was old enough to remember her, Ella was already in her late seventies or maybe early eighties. She was sharp, quick-witted and she didn't smile much, but when she did, her warmth would embrace you. She embodied a spirit of 'lets-get-it-done'. I loved her walk. She kept her shoulders squared, her back ramrod-straight, her head held high and her eyes gazing straight ahead. She exuded confidence and capability. If she decided to support your cause, you knew that it would be a winner.

I would spend time at Ella's house on occasion if my grandmother was too busy working a field where she could not bring the children. I would play with Cousin Ella's grandchildren who might be visiting her that day. Sometimes she would be canning along with her sister who also lived with her, or they would be quilting, working in the garden, or baking. In fact Ella was a bundle of motion and her motto seemed to be 'idle hands invite the devil.'

As she worked Cousin Ella would talk to us about her immediate family. Her husband Fred Reese had passed away many years before. Some of her children had migrated to Wyoming or to other states by the time I met her, but she loved to talk about their accomplishments and show me pictures of her grandchildren.

One of her daughters, OssieMae lived in the area and not too far from her mother. Like her mother, OssieMae was a proud, confident woman but who laughed often and seemed to live life to the fullest. She lived in the moment, but was still patient with children. I remember how OssieMae would always encourage me to speak up for myself and become more assertive. And she would show me how to perform small tasks around the kitchen, like drying dishes, slicing tomatoes, or shelling peas. Both mother and daughter blanketed me with kindness that summer. And although I was still shy and timid at the summer's end, their personalities left a lasting impression on me, like seedlings to be treasured for a lifetime.

AMOS FAMILY *portrait, 2014. Mama at age 89 (Author's collection)*

My mom **MARGIE R. (MAPP) AMOS** and dad **WILLIE J. AMOS**, 1994 (Author's collection)

ALGIA WASH (1934 - 2008) *pictured in early 2000's. Photo from collection of Rochelle Wash and family*

BESSIE WASH, *wife of Algia Wash, 1960s. Photo from collection of Rochelle Wash and family*

ALGIA LEE WASH, *1950s. Photo from collection of Rochelle Wash and family*

DARRYL WASH (1959 - 1970) *son of Algia and Bessie Wash. Photo from collection of Rochelle Wash and family*

LINDSEY MAPP, *father of two daughters, host of grandchildren and great grands. Lived in Newton County until his death in 1990. Photo from collection of Dora Alexander.*

ELBERT MAPP. *father and grandfather to host of descendants. Lived in Newton County until his death in 2007. Photo from the collection of Lindsey D. Mapp.*

MERTIE B.MAPP GOODEN, *Mother of six children, host of grandchildren and descendants. Lived in Detroit MI for several years until her death in 1970. Photo from the collection of Pat Gooden and family*

DELMER GOODEN (c.1920 - 1998), *husband of Mertie B. MAPP. Photo from the collection of Pat Gooden and family*

PEARL MAPP WHITFIELD, *Mother of two sons. Lived in Newton County until her death in 1949. Photo from the collection of Sandra Whitfield Smith.*

Parker WHITFIELD (pictured in youth) *married Pearl MAPP, father of Oscar WHITFIELD. Photo from the collection of Sandra Whitfield Smith.*

OSCAR WHITFIELD, *son of Parker & Pearl MAPP Whitfield. Photo from the collection of Sandra Whitfield Smith.*

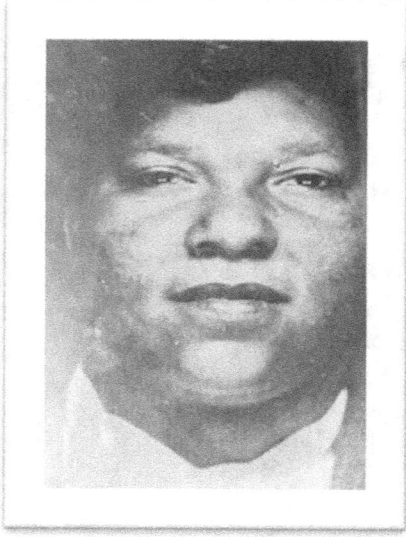

Dorothea Mapp RUSHING *was the mother of one son and leaves a host of grandchildren and descendants. She migrated to Detroit, Michigan in the 1940's, where she lived until her death in 1952. Photo from the collection of* Mary Jo Rushing.

ERA M. DALLAS (c.1921 - 1989) *daughter of Leola MAPP Dallas. Photo from the collection of Arcine Blaylock.*

LINDA A. GOODEN (1947-2011) *daughter of Mertie MAPP Gooden. Photo from the collection of Pat Gooden and family*

BILLY JAMES GOODEN (1945 - 2011), *son of Mertie MAPP Gooden. Photo from the collection of Gooden family*

BILLY JAMES GOODEN, *later in life. Photo from the collection of Gooden family*

ROBERT C. GOODEN, 1950s. *Photo from the collection of Yolanda Gooden.*

ROBERT C. GOODEN (1943 - 2019) *son of Mertie MAPP Gooden. Photo from the collection of Yolanda Gooden.*

My mom and dad **WILLIE AMOS** and **MARGIE (MAPP) AMOS** *as young parents in the 1950s. Photo Courtesy of Will Amos II.*

WILBERT and **DOROTHY SIMS**, *1960s. Photo from the collection of Lucia Sims.*

WOODROW and **FELICIA SIMS**, *1950s. Photo from the collection of Wilbur Sims.*

Clorius (1929 - 1993) and **Ann RUSHING**, *pictured in 1950s. Photo from the collection of Mary Jo Rushing.*

ROBERT CHARLES GOODEN and wife **ANNIE GOODEN**, *1970s. Photo from the collection of Yolanda Gooden.*

CHAPTER 6

The Huddlestons of Newton County – A Major Branch of Our Tribe

During the Civil War, a young enslaved man named John Huddleston worked tirelessly to protect his plantation's livestock from Union soldiers marching with General William Tecumseh Sherman. According to area folklore, he hid the plantation's horses so well that the Union troops, practicing Sherman's harsh "scorched earth" strategy, could not find them to confiscate.

Yet the tiny township of Union, Mississippi, where John Huddleston lived, was spared from destruction. Local oral history claims this was because of the town's name, which may have symbolized loyalty—or at least neutrality—to the Union cause.

After the war, John Huddleston was a young man with newly earned freedom and the heavy challenge of building a life from scratch. He began digging trenches for new roads, later learning the craft of brick-making, which allowed him to earn a steady income. Eventually he started a brick-making business in the area with Dock Viverette, his son-in-law. His discipline and vision eventually enabled him to buy land and establish a new settlement called Spring Hill, named for its abundant freshwater springs.

We found a written narrative about John's life in the *Spring Hill Missionary Baptist Church 150th Anniversary,* published in 2016 by the membership. According to this historical document, by 1866 John founded the church and a school. He wanted to provide a place for children of the formerly enslaved to learn, worship, and gather as a community. Through hard work, optimism, and perseverance, John Huddleston rose to become one of the most prominent Black landowners in the region and was known as the "richest black man in Union." We located a land deed for Newton County showing that John transferred a parcel of land to Spring Hill Church in December 1887.

John lived well into his 90s and witnessed the Great Depression before passing in 1933. We were able to visit his tombstone and grave marker recently in August 2025, which is a well-preserved monument cherished by the Spring Hill community nearly a century after John's death.

DNA research has confirmed connections between my family and John Huddleston's descendants, even though the precise family link remains unclear. John married Mattie Payne McCurdy, and together they had four children, including a daughter named Janie, who married into the Viverette family—relatives who now share DNA with me through my grandfather Mack Huddleston.

So the Huddlestons are Blood

Our search revealed that the Huddleston family tree was far more extensive than we ever imagined. My grandfather Mack Huddleston, his parents, siblings, and extended relatives represented a huge network of relatives.

Another bonus of this genealogy search is that we discovered Mack Huddleston's parents, Jessie and Mary Huddleston, whose names I had not known before.   Records show that Jessie Huddleston married Mary Gardner in 1891 and nine children were born from that union. Born in 1894, Mack Huddleston was the couple's second child.

Mary's family surname Gardner was completely unknown to me before our research. The Gardners also represent a large network of people in Newton County, which is obviously another source of blood relations for me and my children.

Lastly, while looking through some of my mother's keepsakes I discovered a hidden treasure. It was a delicate and faded sympathy card Mack Huddleston had sent to my mother in 1963, honoring the passing of my grandmother Larcine. Mack and my grandmother were never married. Though I don't know if he and Grandmother had much contact over the years prior to her death, that card served as a small token of the connection between the lives of our two grandparents.

Fighting in World War I While Black

By 1917, Mack Huddleston was a young man in his early twenties living in rural Newton County. Like many of his peers, he reported to the draft board in Decatur, Mississippi, and by August 1918 he had enlisted in the U.S. Army. He was soon deployed to France, where he served until July 1919, returning home as a World War I veteran.

History tells us that African American soldiers in World War I faced many hardships and challenges. They were often denied standard uniforms and weapons, relegated to labor duties like digging trenches or burying the dead, and sometimes even forced to bunk in the dark hulls of ships while white soldiers occupied the upper decks.

It was only when French military leaders insisted on their combat participation that Black soldiers were finally armed—ironically, with French weapons. The Harlem Hellfighters (369th Infantry) became famous for their bravery and skill, earning France's highest military honors, while the U.S. Army withheld similar recognition as documented by Francois Reinhardt in his 2017 film *"The Harlem Hellfighters' Great War."*

Returning home, many Black veterans faced racism and violence, with some even lynched for wearing their uniforms. While we have no personal stories from Mack about his war service, his life and longevity stand as a testament to the resilience and courage it took to serve as a Black soldier in Jim Crow America.

⚜ ⚜ ⚜

Mack Huddleston (1894 - 1984), *father of Margie Ree Amos, my grandfather. Photo from the collection of Lynn Hunt.*

Meeting My Grandfather

In November 1963, just as the school year rolled toward Thanksgiving, my seventh-grade class mourned the assassination of President John F. Kennedy. Around the same time, my mother received an unexpected phone call: Mack Huddleston, her biological father, wanted to visit us.

For me, as a pre-teen, it was shocking to learn that my mother's "real dad" was alive. She had never spoken much about him, so I had never imagined him at all. And then, suddenly, there he was, sitting in our living room.

He was short, distinguished-looking, with glasses and a closely shaved haircut. He carried himself with the calm authority of a church dignitary. He was kind, self-assured, and seemed generous, giving us kids quarters or even dollar bills, and handing my mother an envelope I would later understand was a gesture of support.

Grandchildren of Larcina MAPP and Mack HUDDLESTON.
AMOS Family Portrait, 1980 (Author's collection)

Yet I felt conflicted. Where had he been all those years? My mother had lived her entire girlhood without a father, and by the time he came into our lives, she had ten children of her own.

Time, however, is a remarkable healer. Over the years, we grew to accept and cherish our grandfather. I visited him several times when I was a college student, spending precious time with him before his health declined. He eventually passed away in 1984, and by that time as a younger adult I had become very grateful for the unexpected gift of having spent those years with my grandfather.

Mack Huddleston's Later Life

After the war, Mack returned to Mississippi, living a life defined by hard work, community, and family. He relocated from Newton County to Jackson, Mississippi, where he married Hattie Lee Tabron, his lifelong partner. The couple had no biological children together.

Mack Huddleston had fathered two daughters in his youth with two separate mothers, being unmarried to either. My mother's half-sister, Hattie Mae, married and moved away from Newton County while my mother was a teen. The two half-sisters never had the opportunity to spend very much time together, but they knew each other growing up. By reaching out to some relatives found through Ancestry.com I was able to trace some of Hattie Mae's descendants with whom I have begun to develop relationships.

Mack's later years were spent as a respected family elder, World War I veteran, and a vibrant participant in community life, including the American Legion and VFW.

Mack Huddleston passed away in 1984, having lived a full life and having endured many experiences. He had seen war and peace, survived the Great Depression and experienced the hope for a better life ushered in by the Civil Rights Movement. He left behind a legacy which I hope this narrative will help spread to future generations.

CHAPTER 7

Migration Journeys: "A Change is Gonna Come"

"By the time the Great Migration was over, few Americans had not been touched by it... perhaps the most significant measure... was the act of leaving itself, regardless of the individual outcome... The achievement was in making the decision to be free and acting on that decision..."

—Isabel Wilkerson, The Warmth of Other Suns, 2010

Aunt Corine: Chicago Trailblazer

Aunt Corine. Bold, independent, and outspoken. Her outer beauty only scratched the surface of her giant personality. Practical and resourceful, she canned and pickled vegetables, was a quilt-maker, and even raised pigs for sale. She could handle a rifle, hunt if she needed to, and was a natural-born leader and survivor. I remember her infectious laugh, even back when I was a little girl. I also remember how she was known for her 'don't take no stuff' reputation. She was known for being very capable of defending herself, be it another female or even a male enemy.

CORINA MAPP WASH, *Daughter of Charlie and Mary Mapp. Mother of two sons and host of grandchildren and descendants. She was pioneer of the Great Migration to Chicago in the 1950s. Photo from collection of Rochelle Wash and family*

Aunt Corine had a flair for beauty and art that stretched beyond the farm. She designed and crafted stunning hats for church and social occasions—beautiful and elegant pieces that my mother loved and had told us about. Aunt Corine's spirit, I would guess, may have been a little too large for the red clay roads of 1950s Newton County. That spirit led her to venture out to experience another world like going 'up North' would offer.

So around 1957 or 1958, she took a leap of faith and boarded a train bound for Chicago, leaving her home in Mississippi. For nearly 15 years, she faced the biting wind of the "Hawk," the nickname for Chicago's infamous winter weather. She learned to navigate a world where Northern racism may have been quieter, but still restricting. Like other African-American women who migrated North she was likely limited to domestic jobs at first, and no doubt endured the subtle racial slights that came with that work. Black migrants also had to live in certain areas of the city, which were usually the worst areas. But compared to the daily humiliations and sometimes dangers of Jim Crow Mississippi, the sense of freedom may have been worth the tradeoff.

I remember how Aunt Corine would mail packages to my mother, and how we children would race to the door when we heard there was a "box from Chicago." I couldn't imagine what the city looked like; in my mind, it was like Oz, with streets paved in gold. Each box was like magic. Sometimes there was candy, sometimes clothes, sometimes just odds and ends—but none of that mattered. The thrill was that she had sent us treasures from the faraway, glittering world called Chicago.

I was in high school, maybe a junior or a rising senior when Aunt Corine returned to Mississippi for good. My mother simply announced one day, "Aunt Corine is back." That fall in 1968, my mother, my sister, and our neighborhood best friend boarded the Greyhound bus to go visit Newton County. I had not been there in several years. But we were all so excited to get to see our Auntie.

We experienced one other small victory and cause for celebration that day. Due to the Civil Rights Act which had passed since our last bus ride to Newton County, we could now sit anywhere on the bus, walk freely through the terminals, and not be subjected to the vile "Colored" or "White Only" water fountain signs that had been markers of Jim Crow.

When we arrived at her house, Aunt Corine was her usual self: vibrant, witty, and full of laughter. She slipped back into Newton County life as though she had never left. And her confidence had only been boosted by her experiences up North. Aunt Corine was back, only now she was even better.

Going West: Family Pioneers in Wyoming

Not all of our family chose the industrial North. Some went west, chasing opportunity in places that seemed, at first glance, unlikely for Black folks born in the South. Places like Texas, Oklahoma, and California saw their share of our relatives. But the biggest surprise came from those who chose to settle in Wyoming.

"Casper, Wyoming" by name alone brings up images of a cowboy town in a Hollywood film. Wyoming, especially in the 1950s, would appear to be a world where people who looked like us, Black folks, did not exist. But the real history of the West tells a different story.

One of the first all-black towns in the American West was called Empire, Wyoming, founded by formerly enslaved people in 1908. Empire was a village of sixty-five black-owned farms, but unfortunately it had to be abandoned by 1930 due to economic hardship and racial violence.

Our Mapp and Huddleston family members migrated to Wyoming decades later, in the 1940s and early 1950s. We don't know if the two groups collaborated in any way. However, some came for military service at the newly established Casper Army Air Base, like my mother's cousin Gaddis Reese, grandson of Coleman Mapp. Others sought work in the oil fields, coal mines, or local service jobs.

GADDIS REESE, *WWII Veteran, son of Ella MAPP Reese, grandson of Coleman MAPP. Photo from Amos Family collection, passed down from our grandmother Larcine Mapp Whitfield*

Life was still hard, and danger was never far away. Some family members endured traumatic incidents, including shootings and domestic violence, in that remote environment. In the Casper Morning Star, November 3, 1954 newspaper article we find reported the shooting death of J. V. Mapp, age 21, in a domestic dispute.

Yet they stayed. They adjusted to a place where few would have imagined Black Southerners could thrive. Over time, their children and grandchildren became teachers, ministers, military servicemembers, and other professionals. They built lives that defied the odds, contributing to a region that was not always welcoming. Our relatives proved that by determination, hard work, and love for family that their struggles made a difference, paving the way for future generations.

North to Flint, Michigan

Even before the Great Migration swelled in the 1940s, some family members saw promise in the booming auto industry of Michigan. The town of Flint became a key destination for the Mapp and Huddleston families, preceding their migration to Detroit, Flint's neighbor and 'big sister'.

Benjamin "Ben" Mapp, born in the 1880s in Newton County, was among the first to leave. By 1919, he and his wife, Emma, had settled in Flint, where he began work in the auto industry. By the 1920s, census and city directory records list Ben as first a laborer and later a skilled factory worker—a small but critical step toward economic stability.

Emma Mapp, determined in her own right, earned a Nursing Diploma from the American Red Cross in 1925, joining thirty other Black women whose names appeared in the Flint Journal. Her training allowed her to work in hospitals, clinics, or private homes—a remarkable achievement in an era when most Black women were relegated to domestic labor. That diploma represented not just employment, but dignity and independence.

Sadly, both Emma and Ben died young, in their 50s. By the time Ben passed in 1934, he was listed as a widower, his daughter Allie Morgan serving as the informant for his death certificate. That document connects him directly to our family's Mississippi roots, naming Harriette and Richard Mapp as his parents.

Other relatives followed, like Green B. Huddleston, the son of Prince and grandson of Harriette Mapp. Green migrated to Flint around 1917, decades ahead of the main wave of Black migration. He spent nearly 40 years at the Buick factory retiring in 1956, and was a proud member of the United Auto Workers union. He lived in Flint for six decades, but like many of our people, he ultimately returned home in death, having been buried in Newton County, resting alongside generations of family who never left the South.

My own migration story began in the 1970s. After high school I attended a four-year college in Southern Illinois and earned a Bachelor's degree in Sociology and Community Studies. Through my college friends I had some exposure to life in the big cities of St Louis and Chicago. I got to visit those places by going home with friends for Thanksgiving, Spring Breaks and other weekend trips.

Even though I had enjoyed the big city visits, initially my mindset was to return home to Mississippi after graduation to begin my career. But once I returned home, my real life experiences did not measure up to my dreams and expectations. First of all, just in general I had been naive about the job market but quickly discovered that my degree did not prepare me with any specific job skills. So the jobs I qualified for were totally dead-end and I could see no future in them. Or I would have to wait years for any chance of advancement. Not to mention the routine micro-aggressions and subtle racism which I witnessed on a daily basis in the workplace. Unfortunately, I had to postpone my plans for settling down back in Mississippi since the employment scene was so dismal. So just like that, when my Northern cousins came South a few weeks later, I hitched a ride back to Detroit with them.

In the 70s Detroit was still a beautiful place for Black families to live, even though most of that was changing drastically by the 1980s. For the moment though I became a wannabe Detroiter and Northerner. After working retail and staying in my sister's extra bedroom, I eventually got a job with a government agency which allowed me to get my own apartment and a car. When not working I enjoyed leisure life as a young twenty-something going to parties, shopping, and spending summer afternoons in the lively, lush, Belle Isle Park.

By the mid-seventies I realized I wanted more from life and began to explore spirituality, eventually converting to the religion of Islam. I also went back to school to work toward an advanced degree in my field. I met a like-minded young man who had also migrated to Detroit from the South and we married in 1977. After the birth of our first two children, we decided to return to his hometown in Memphis, Tennessee.

Prior to leaving Detroit, I had completed an internship in Student Services at the University of Michigan, Dearborn and a Master's Degree in Education Administration at Wayne State University. It wasn't easy to pack up and leave the life we had made for ourselves but the draw of being closer to family, and the prospect of providing a more relaxed environment for raising our children eventually won us over. We left Michigan in the summer of 1980 just a few short weeks following my graduation, and like so many other African-Americans, I too experienced reverse-migration.

"Homecoming"

From Newton County to Chicago, Wyoming, or to Flint, Michigan our family's migrations tell a story larger than our own. They are part of the Great Migration and the broader African-American experience in the

United States. Our family's migrations were mostly a pursuit of freedom, opportunity, and dignity within a system of racial discrimination.

Whether our ancestors braved the icy "Hawk" in Chicago, the dust and isolation of Wyoming, or the auto factories in Flint, they carried with them the same legacy—a determination to carve out a life beyond the narrow limits that Mississippi tried to impose on them.

But no matter how far they went, there was no substitute for the beauty of the land, the generosity of spirit in the community, and the love among family left behind. Migration took them far away, but in spirit many longed for the warmth and majesty of being home, and for those who never made it back physically, there were memories, hopes, and dreams.

In many cases people were brought back to Newton County for burial, for their final resting place. This was a family tradition which was very prevalent from the 1920s through the 1970s, but has trickled down even until the present day.

CHAPTER 8

Summary and Reflections

"History, despite its wrenching pain, cannot be unlived, but if faced with courage need not be lived again."

—Maya Angelou

As we uncovered more about our family history, we began to realize that we have more questions than answers. Each mystery solved seemed to create more mysteries. For instance, it is unclear as to what happened to force Harriette to sell her land. But the biggest disappointment is that we have little evidence to show how and when Harriette died. She simply vanished from records after the 1910 US Census. When added to the unfortunate circumstance that there were very few family stories passed down about her, it feels like her later life was shrouded in mystery.

What we learned about our ancestors, and especially about Harriette, is that her life was filled with *interruptions,* but which she ultimately overcame. Harriette faced unimaginable obstacles during her lifetime, but she constantly rose to the challenge.

First, Harriette is described by the census takers as being a 'mulatto'. A mulatto is a term used in the 1800's to categorize a mixed race person, usually meaning having a black and a white parent. To historians it also indicates a possible rape of Harriette's mother by a white landowner or plantation overseer.

Secondly, Harriette's first three children are also 'mulatto'. On her first son Prince's death certificate, a slaveholder, Ben Huddleston is identified as Prince's father.

Therefore a likely pattern was established with Harriette's mother which continued with her daughter. It would not be unreasonable to speculate that some landowner, slaveholder fathered Harriette's first child. Very likely through coercion as she would have been a young teen at the time of her child's birth.

Third, by the time Harriette is twenty years old or so, she is forced to migrate from Georgia to the state of Mississippi, which means she likely had to leave behind her mother and any other family members who were present in her life at that time, such as siblings, aunts, uncles, etc. She had to experience and endure the trauma of being torn from her entire family line. Such is an example of a brutal *interruption* carried out by one human family and executed on another human family without regard for the enslaved family's humanity.

But Harriette took those circumstances in stride and raised her children in the new environment, making sure that they had shelter, food, were educated and instilled in them a strong faith in God.

Finally, once Harriette has been able to somehow adjust and make a life for herself as a freedwoman, her marriage to a soulmate and father to her children comes to an abrupt end. Her husband, Richard disappears suddenly by 1870, which leads our research to speculate that something nefarious may have occurred, like a lynching.

We do have records to indicate that Richard was an organizer, one who took the lead to demand that workers be paid their wages, as indicated by records from the Freedman's Bureau archives. Also Mississippi State Voter Registration rolls from 1867 indicate that Richard was a voter. Apparently, Harriette's husband was socially conscious and an activist to some extent during his time. And although his and Harriette's dreams are interrupted by white supremacy, they taught their children to work hard, to bond together in family love, and to remain grounded in faith.

Harriette's story is not uncommon among African-Americans when we research our family histories. There were millions of formerly enslaved people whose lives were cut short, stunted, traumatized by the conditions of chattel slavery, Reconstruction, and Jim Crow laws. The trajectory of our "inalienable rights" promised by the US Constitution was never grasped and held by my great-great grandmother. Despite her obvious fortitude, her being industrious as a landowner herself, her spirit of survival, her legacy had been obscured.

Because of the sheer inhumanity of the government she was subjected to in her time, her life became a series of interruptions which prevented her story and her generational wealth from being passed on to her family.

However, the legacy of her identity, her character, her strength, her survival instincts, her spirit, and her humanity is what matters most. And her legacy is what this book hopes to begin to restore. Her courage, determination, and her spirit are her legacy which we wish to pass on to future generations.

Beyond the strength, character, determination and courage displayed by many of our ancestors they were also part of a community which embodied love and support for each other. These qualities far exceed simply having wealth, or worse forsaking family love and humanity in the pursuit of wealth.

The entire state of Mississippi is composed of communities like the ones where my grandparents and ancestors lived and survived. I can visualize a change for the state on the near horizon. A change that began with so many African-Americans who refused to roll over and give up in the face of white supremacy and state-sponsored discrimination. African-Americans were always determined to educate their children and to strengthen their young with faith and family love. Our people went to high school and on to college even as Jim Crow laws prevented them from sitting at the front of a bus or eating in the dining room of a restaurant. For example, my own mother boarded with a relative twenty miles away from home so that she could attend and graduate from high school. That was because her local school only went to eighth grade. My mother also attended college in 1947.

Our ancestors endured the worst of discrimination but vowed not to be defeated. Today more young people are attending college, obtaining degrees, and entering professions as a result of the examples set by our ancestors. More entrepreneurs, businesses, and industries are being created by their descendants.

The changes in the state of Mississippi will accommodate the humanity of all citizens, will reward hard work and dedication, and will encompass diversity. It will no longer be acceptable to live in a society where the wealth is concentrated in the hands of just a few, like a society of lords and serfs, bishops and pawns. A new society of faith, hope, and inclusion will rule. And the new dawn will be led by today's youth, under whose leadership the world will see a rebirth, a renaissance in Mississippi and likewise in this nation.

EPILOGUE

Family Reunion 2025

People came from thousands of miles, from California, Texas, New York, Chicago or closer locations, like Atlanta, Kentucky, and the Gulf Coast. In 1978 when our very first reunion kicked off, many family members made a 16-hour road trip from Detroit or Cleveland. Today, more people fly into New Orleans and rent a car or choose the nearest airport at Jackson.

Back in the day there may have been a little bragging going on, showing off the Cadillac or the new '79 Bonneville. Our family has always been loud and proud, boisterous, loving. So many cousins, all the hugs, smiles, and great bursts of laughter. I think we all had missed this gathering. Due to the pandemic of 2020, we had not been able to meet like this for the past five years.

This year's theme was 'Harlem Nights, the Roaring 20s'. Ladies bedazzled in pearls and feathers, flapper skirts, sequins and lace. And the men were not to be outdone with their crisp, white shirts, black bowties and black armbands, their fedoras, looking handsome and debonair. What a gorgeous crowd! And if the teenagers did their own thing, sticking to their jeans and t-shirts, nobody worried.

The deejay played music from 1960s blues to current-day hip-hop and top 10 hits. The food and beverages were plentiful and were being enjoyed by all.

The magic of the night was so obvious and felt by everyone in the vicinity. Even the building itself, the local American Legion, felt refurbished, with walls and floors gleaming, and perhaps new lighting. People were beaming, with old family connections being revived and new relationships being built. Old 'beef' seems to have been forgotten, or at least set aside for the weekend. There were people there I had not seen in over five, ten, or twenty years. My daughter had a chance to get to know cousins and aunties that she had not seen since her childhood days.

My grandchildren had a chance to experience walking on the grounds where their ancestors walked, a chance to meet the people who are their blood.

A highpoint of the evening was celebrating each branch of the family by acknowledging all the descendants of our great-grandparents, Charlie and Mary Mapp. Their survivors represented ten family groupings. This gigantic family tree was honored by taking family pictures of the respective groups. These ten 'tribes' symbolized the strength and unity which can be grasped when families come together and support each other. Our unity and strength also represent the promise of family pride and family prosperity, the promise of a new day, a renaissance in a place called Mississippi.

ENDNOTES

[1] Huie, William Bradford. "The Shocking Story of Approved Killing in Mississippi. Look Magazine, January 1956.

[2] Mars, Florence. Witness in Philadelphia. Louisiana State University Press. 1977. p.262.

[3] Booker, Simeon and Carol McCabe Booker. Shocking the Conscience: A Reporter's Account of the Civil Rights Movement. University Press of Mississippi. 2013. P. 94.

[4] Scarsella, Jameson. "Deion Sanders' Lasting Impact on HBCU Football Programs" businessdownload.com 29 March 2024.

IN MEMORIAM

My mother **Margie R. Amos** *(July 4, 1925 - September 11, 2016).*
Photo courtesy of Wilbur Sims

WILLIE J. AMOS, *my dad (May 12, 1922 – November 20, 1997) (Author's collection)*

DARRYL M. AMOS, *my brother (1961 - 1992). Photo from Amos family collection*

KAREEM B. COWAN (1983 - 2003), *author's son (Author's collection)*

RICK AMOS, *author's brother (1963 - 2017) Photo from Amos Family collection*

MARILYN AMOS JOHNSON, *author's youngest sister (1968 - 2018) Photo from Amos Family collection*

DENNIS R. AMOS, *author's brother, (1957 - 2021) (Author's collection)*

LARCINA MAPP WHITFIELD's *gravesite at Saint Hill Church Cemetery, Newton County Mississippi. Photos courtesy of Jimmy E. Amos*

BIBLIOGRAPHY

1.   Amos, Tanisha N. The Mapp Family Directory Guide. 2008.

2.   Baptist, Edward E. The Half Has Never Been Told: Slavery and the Making of American Capitalism. Basic Books, 2014.

3.   Barnwell, Marion, editor. A Place Called Mississippi: Collected Narratives. University Press of Mississippi, 1997.

4.   Booker, Simeon, and Carol McCabe Booker. Shocking the Conscience: A Reporter's Account of the Civil Rights Movement. University Press of Mississippi, 2013.

5.   Brown, J. A. History of Newton County, 1834–1894.

6.   Collier, Melvin J. Mississippi to Africa: A Journey of Discovery. Heritage Books, 2008.

7.   DuBois, W.E.B. Black Reconstruction In America, 1860-1880. Simon & Schuster, The Free Press edition, 1998.

8.   Eubanks, W. Ralph. Ever Is a Long Time: A Journey Into Mississippi's Dark Past. Perseus Books, 2003.

9.   Evers, Charles, and Andrew Szanton. Have No Fear: The Charles Evers Story. John Wiley & Sons, 1997.

10.   Field, Kendra Taira. Growing Up with the Country. Yale University Press, 2018.

11.   Foster, Robin R. My Best Genealogy Tips: Finding Formerly Enslaved Ancestors. Benjamin Book Publishing, 2022.

12.   Garland, Emily Allen. Giving a Voice to the Ancestors. 1990s?

13.   Garrett-Nelson, LaBrenda. "An Enslaved Person's FAN Club." Florida State Genealogical Society webinar, 19 June 2025.

14.   Gates, Henry Louis, editor. Classic Slave Narratives. Penguin Putnam, 1987.

15.   Georgia Department of Archives and History. 1850 Census of Georgia (Greene County), compiled by Rhea Cumming Otto.

16.   Knox, Constance Henley. "How to Search the 1950 Census Before It's Indexed." Genealogy TV, YouTube, 2022.

17.   Lee, Devon Noel. "Mastering the Story Arc in Family History." Family History Fanatics, www.familyhistoryfanatics.com/family-history-story-arc.

18.   Lussana, Sergio A. My Brother Slaves: Friendship, Masculinity, and Resistance in the Antebellum South. University Press of Kentucky, 2016.

19.   Mayo, Ida Mapp. "Mapp Family Reunion Booklet" c. 1978.

20.   McInniss, Jarvis. Afterlives of the Plantation. https://a.co/d/3OhVUuM.

21.   Miller, Derek. Minority Soldiers Fighting in World War I. Cavendish Square, 2018.

22.   Mitchell, Dennis. A New History of Mississippi. University Press of Mississippi, 2014.

23.   Ports, Michael A. Georgia Free Persons of Color. Vols. I–V, 2015.

24.   Reid, Joy-Ann. Medgar & Myrlie: Medgar Evers and the Love Story That Awakened America. Mariner/HarperCollins, 2024.

25.   Reinhardt, Francois. "The Harlem Hellfighters' Great War-History Documentary." 2017.

26.   Slocum, Karla. Black Towns, Black Futures: The Enduring Allure of a Black Place in the American West. University of North Carolina Press, 2019.

27.   Smith, Farrah. Viverette Family Directory. 2011.

28.   Smith, Robyn N. "A Beginner's Guide to Using Court Records." Reclaiming Kin, reclaimingkin.com.

29.   Smith-Sewell, Nicka. "The Trifecta: The Secret to Researching the Formerly Enslaved." Webinar: National Black Authors, March 2023.

30.   Smith-Sewell, Nicka. "The Ultimate Family History Interview Primer." June 2015. www.whoisnickasmith.com.

31.   Taylor, Amy Murrell. Embattled Freedom: Journeys through the Civil War's Slave Refugee Camps. University of North Carolina Press. 2018 edition.

32.   Taulbert, Clifton. Once Upon a Time When We Were Colored. Council Oaks Books, 1989.

33.   Thompson, Wright. The Barn: The Secret History of a Murder in Mississippi. Penguin Press, 2024.

34.   Ward, Jesmyn. Let Us Descend. Scribner Press. 2023.

35.   Wells, Ida B. Crusade for Justice: The Autobiography of Ida B. Wells. Edited by Alfreda M. Duster, University of Chicago Press, 1970, 2020.

36.   West, Elizabeth J. Finding Francis: One Family's Journey from Slavery to Freedom. University of South Carolina Press, 2022.

37.   White, Sherwood, et al. Greene County, Georgia 1786–1876.

38.   Wikipedia contributors. "Newton County, Mississippi." Wikipedia, https://en.wikipedia.org/wiki/Newton_County,_Mississippi.

39.   Wilkerson, Isabel. The Warmth of Other Suns: The Epic Story of America's Great Migration. Random House, 2010.

40.   "Treaty of Dancing Rabbit Creek." Wikipedia, https://en.wikipedia.org/wiki/Treaty_of_Dancing_Rabbit_Creek.

Front Cover Photo Credits

1. Top row left: from collection of Wilbur Sims
2. Top row right: from collection of Mary Jo Rushing
3. Middle row left: from collection of Wilbur Sims
4. Middle row center: from Amos Family archives
5. Middle row right: from collection of Claudia Jones
6. Bottom Row left: from collection of Lucia Sims
7. Bottom Row center: from collection of Pat Gooden
8. Bottom Row right: from collection of Rochelle Wash

REFERENCES

Chapter 3

1900 US Federal Census. Newton County MS. Harriette Mapp household. Digital image. Ancestry. com

Newton county MS Chancery Clerk. Deed Book 5. 20March1882. Digital image. FamilySearch.org

MS Secretary of State Educable Children Lists. Newton County. 1885. Digital image. FamilySearch.org

Newton County MS Chancery Clerk Deed Book 11. 15December1890. Digital image. FamilySearch.org

Texas, US Death Certificates, 1903-1982. Roxie {Watter} Walton.
18July1941. Ancestry.com

Chapter 4

Newton County MS Circuit Court Clerk Marriages, vol.2. Charlie Mapp and Mary Jefferson. 27December1894. Digital image. FamilySearch.org

1920 US Federal Census. Newton County MS. Charlie Mapp household. Digital image. Ancestry.com

Newton County MS Circuit Court Clerk Marriages, vol.2. Charlie Mapp and Gracy Cleveland. 24March1887. Digital image. FamilySearch.org

Newton County MS Circuit Court Clerk Marriages, vol.1.

Coleman Mapp and Frances Cleveland. 14February1884. Digital image. FamilySearch.org

MS Vital Health Records. Certificate of Death. Coleman M. Mapp. 20April1950. Parents listed as Harriette Huddleston and Richard W. Mapp

1940 US Federal Census. Newton County MS. Joseph Wilson household. Digital image. Ancestry.com

MS Vital Health Records. Certificate of Death. Prince Huddleston. 7July1941. Parents listed as Harriette Huddleston and Richard W. Mapp. Informant: J.H. Wilson

Michigan Department of Health. Certificate of Death. Benjamin Mapp. 2December1934. Parents listed as Harriette Williams Mapp and Richard Mapp. Informant: Allie Morgan

MS Vital Health Records. Certificate of Death. George Mapp. 12April1954. Mother listed as Harriette Mapp

1920 United States Federal Census. Washington Parish LA. Cleve Harris household.   Ancestry.com
https://share.google/W15YAcV5VBnJqcJ3P

Barnett, Jim. "Great Southern Lumber's William Sullivan began Aggressive Reforestation at Bogalusa. "July 17, 2017. LaForestry.com

Chapter 5

1910 US Federal Census. Charlie Mapp household. Newton County MS.

Newton County MS Circuit Court Clerk Marriages. William E. Whitfield and Larcenia (Mapp) Henderson. 26 January 1948. Digital image. FamilySearch.org

Chapter 7

"30 Colored Nurses to Get Diplomas From Red Cross." The Flint Journal. March 20 1925. p.3. www.newspapers.com/image

Kopf, Sy. "Youth's Death Leaves Hollow Spot in Family." Casper Morning Star. November 3, 1954. www.newspapers.com/image